AMERICAN SACRED MUSIC

THREE CENTURIES OF AMERICAN MUSIC

A Collection of American Sacred and Secular Music

Volume 7

Martha Furman Schleifer
Sam Dennison
General Editors

AMERICAN SACRED MUSIC

Edited by
Philip Vandermeer

G.K. HALL & CO.
1991

ISBN 0-8161-0484-0 (set)
0-8161-0542-1 (vol. 1)
0-8161-0543-X(vol. 2)
0-8161-0544-8 (vol. 3)
0-8161-0545-6 (vol. 4)
0-8161-0546-4 (vol. 5)
0-8161-0547-2 (vol. 6)
0-8161-0548-0 (vol. 7)
0-8161-0549-9 (vol. 8)
0-8161-0550-2 (vol. 9)
0-8161-0551-0 (vol. 10)
0-8161-0552-9 (vol. 11)
0-8161-0553-7 (vol. 12)

Contents

Series Preface

The significant rise in interest in the enormous body of American music has resulted in a growing need for study and performance materials. Musicologists and teachers are too often placed in the position of having to deal with genres and styles of American music without having available music examples from the past. *Three Centuries of American Music,* a multiple-volume collection of sacred and secular music, meets this need for academic institutions, scholars, teachers, professional musicians, and amateur performers interested in our musical heritage. The volumes are devoted to what is often called "cultivated," as opposed to "vernacular," music; ethnic, or folk, music is not included.

Each volume has a contributing editor, selected for his or her expertise. The contributing editors have been allowed wide latitude in choosing the examples to be included in each volume. The aim is for the entire series to strike a reasonable balance among the various genres, while including as much as possible that is significant in the vast panorama of American music. The major portion of each volume consists of materials not readily available and some works never before published; well-known works that form an important part of the fabric of American musical culture have also been included. The decision to present most of these materials in facsimile rather than edited, re-engraved form was based on the belief that this would provide primary sources as well as invaluable insights into the state of sheet-music presentation – style, printing, engraving, and so forth – at the time the works were produced.

This series is a beginning in the systematic collection of American music that is often discussed but seldom seen or heard. As such it is certain to arouse discussion among those who use it. We welcome suggestions, corrections, and critical comments from our readers.

We wish to thank the staff of the Music Department and the Fleisher Collection of the Free Library of Philadelphia for providing the majority of music examples in this series. Other libraries, including the Library of Congress, New York Public Library, Harvard University Library, the Historical Society of Pennsylvania, and private collectors provided invaluable assistance in making material available.

Martha Furman Schleifer
Sam Dennison
GENERAL EDITORS

Introduction to Volume 7

1. Early Psalmody

On 18 April 1721 the Reverend Cotton Mather (1663-1728) preached a sermon from his pulpit at Boston's First Church. The biblical text on which he based the sermon was Ephesians 5:19, in which the Apostle Paul admonishes the church to speak "to yourselves in psalms and hymns and spiritual songs, singing and making melodies in your heart to the Lord." In explicating the text Mather pointed out that singing is

> recommended by the Practice of the People of God in all ages; Before, under, and since the Mosaick Dispensation. It is a Duty of many noble and excellent Characters. It is the united Employment of our best Powers, and Passions, in a most regular and perfect Manner, for the highest and most worthy ends. It is public, and solemn Hommage to God and an open Profession of our Allegiance to Him before Men; By which means His declarative Glory is singularly promoted.[1]

This ringing endorsement should put to rest any idea that music was disallowed in Puritan New England. And Mather's attitude was not untraditional; the first book published in the colonies was a psalter commonly called the *Bay Psalm Book*, to which both Mather's grandfathers John Cotton (1584-1642) and Richard Mather (1569-1669) contributed. But the roots of American psalm singing are in Europe, so a proper study of New England church music must begin in the Old World.

The beliefs and practices of the Puritans of England and New England were based on the work of the French reformer John Calvin (1509-64). Like Martin Luther, Calvin based his theology on biblical precepts. There were, of course, important differences in the views of the two men, most often manifested in the different liturgies. One commentator summarizes these differences eloquently: "Luther will have what is not specifically condemned by the Scriptures; whilst Calvin will have only what is ordained by God in the Scriptures."[2]

Calvin, though not a musician, perceived music's power to affect human emotion and behavior and "agreed with the ancient theological concept of the divine origins of music."[3] In his view, music was an effective means of praise, which as a gift of God should be used in worship. Scripture was always the source for musical texts; the music itself was not allowed to overpower the communication of the scripture. Inessential elements were pared away; complex polyphony was discarded in favor of simple melodies; instruments that could overwhelm the voices were forbidden. The texts were most often psalms and canticles translated into the vernacular, and the music was not difficult. Trained choirs were not used; the entire congregation participated in the musical life of the church.

Calvin's precedent was scripture. He tried assiduously to apply Paul's admonitions that churches should "sing with voice and heart" and that spiritual songs are a medium "by which the godly may mutually edify one another."[4] As Calvin proclaimed in his *Institutes of the Christian Religion,* "Since the glory of God ought, in a measure, to shine in the several parts of our bodies, it is especially fitting that the tongue has been assigned and destined for this task, both through singing and through speaking. For it was peculiarly created to tell and proclaim the praise of God."[5] Calvin applied his restrictions to music only within the context of the church; he did not object to other types of music outside the church, as many have thought. As he wrote in his commentary on the book of Genesis, "Now, although the invention of the harp, and of similar instruments of music may minister to our pleasure, rather than to our necessity, still it is not to be thought altogether superfluous; much less does it deserve to be condemned."[6]

Yet as a reformer Calvin was concerned with past abuses. He understood the struggles of the early church fathers, noting their solutions and failures. In the section of his *Institutes* titled "Church Singing," he summarized the opinions of St. Augustine:

> And surely, if the singing be tempered to that gravity which is fitting in the sight of God and the angels, it both lends dignity and grace to sacred actions and has the greatest value in kindling our heart to a true zeal and eagerness to pray. Yet we should be very careful that our ears be not more attentive to the melody than our minds to the spiritual meaning of the words. Augustine also admits in another place that he was so disturbed by the danger that he sometimes wished to see established the custom observed by Athanasius, who ordered the reader to use so little inflection of the voice that he would sound more like a speaker than a singer. But when he recalled how much benefit singing had brought him, he inclined to the other side. Therefore, when this moderation is maintained, it is without any doubt a most holy and salutary practice. On the other hand, such songs as have been composed only for sweetness and delight of the ear are unbecoming to the majesty of the church and cannot but displease God in the highest degree.[7]

Calvin, like Augustine, decided that "reform of singing rather than its rejection"[8] was the appropriate response.

The practical manifestation of Calvin's theological model for church singing is the metrical psalm. These are verse paraphrases of biblical psalms in the vernacular set to popular or folk tunes'[9] using standard meters. Each text is identified by its corresponding meter, depending on the number of syllables for each line of the stanza. In this way the same tune can be used for any text with a corresponding meter. These psalms fit well into Calvin's conception of a reformed church music. Their being "simple," "popular," and "biblical" made it possible for the Reformed congregation, musical or not, to join together in a form of worship that, according to Calvin's reading of scripture was pleasing to God.

The psalter *Aulcuns pseaulmes et cantiques mys en chant* (Strasbourg, 1593) marked Calvin's first published attempt to systematize his theories. The eighteen psalm settings and three canticles, selected from Clement Marot's *Trente pseaulmes*[10] and Calvin's own translations, were specifically designed to "edify good souls." Even though the melodies were generally unascribed, several can be traced to earlier Strasbourg songbooks and two can be attributed to Matthias Greiter, a local musician.[11]

The *Aulcuns pseaulmes* paved the way for subsequent psalters. Theodore de Bèze added new versifications to the repertory, and new melodies, such as the "Old 100," were composed by Loys (Louis) Bourgeouis. In 1562 a new Calvinist psalter was published in its complete form as *Les pseaulmes mis en rime françoise, par Clement Marot & Theodore de Bèze.*[12] It contained 150 psalms, 2 canticles, and 125 different melodies. *Les pseaulmes* enjoyed widespread popularity in France and Switzerland; twenty-four printers produced tens of thousands of copies in Paris alone. The psalter provided the model for most subsequent monophonic psalters, including those in England, Scotland, and, indirectly, America.[13] While it is beyond the scope of this brief introduction to provide a comprehensive history of Scottish and English psalmody,[14] let it simply be said that the first psalters in New England were, directly or indirectly, British imports.

Among the various goods and supplies carried by the one hundred or so Pilgrims,[15] Puritan (Calvinist) separatists, who landed in Plymouth, Massachusetts, in 1620 aboard the famed ship *Mayflower* were copies of Henry Ainsworth's *The Book of Psalms: Englished Both in Prose and Metre*. Ainsworth (1570-1623) was an English minister and scholar renowned for his commentaries on the Hebrew Old Testament.[16] As one of the first Puritan religious exiles to flee to Holland (in 1593), he assumed a leadership role in a principal congregation in Amsterdam.[17] Though Ainsworth did not accompany the Pilgrims to the New World, his psalter became a vital aspect of the Plymouth community. Ainsworth's *Book of Psalms* was first published in 1612 in Amsterdam. Through the next six editions it proved to be a scholarly work containing music of great melodic and rhythmic variety. Thirty-nine melodies were included and, in Gilbert Chases's words, "only a few . . . use the four-line ballad stanza (so-called 'common meter') that later became so tiresomely prevalent in English psamlody."[18]

English Puritanism was an attempt to "purify" the Anglican church by purging it of all vestiges of Roman Catholicism and molding it into a form similar to continental Reformed Puritanism (Calvinism). The Pilgrims, with their more radical separatist attitudes, left Britain altogether. More moderate Puritans tried to work within the British system. Eventually they gained a majority in Parliament and in 1628 passed legislation significantly checking the king's power. By 1629 Charles I regained his power, dissolved Parliament, and tacitly approved persecution of the Puritans. It was at this time that the main migration of Puritans to the New World began. By the end of 1630 over two thousand had settled in the Massachusetts Bay Colony; by 1643 two hundred ships had transported twenty thousand people.[19]

The psalter of choice for Puritan immigrants who came to the United States directly from England to establish the Massachusetts Bay Colony in 1629 was *The Whole Booke of Psalmes Collected into English Meter*, by Thomas Sternhold, John Hopkins, and others. "Sternhold and Hopkins," as it is commonly called, became the standard for English-speaking Protestants. Six hundred editions were published between 1562 and 1828.[20] The book contains the 150 psalms translated into English verse. The great majority are in common meter (four lines alternating eight and six syllables respectively, abbreviated 8.6.8.6.). Ballad meter, as this meter is also known, was frequently used in popular ballads of the day, hence placing the psalms within the populist theological framework that governed the Puritan church.[21] Some editions of Sternhold and Hopkins contained music. Tunes in common use could have provided music for the psalms, and *The Whole Booke of Psalmes*, Thomas Ravenscroft's collection of ninety-seven harmonized psalm tunes, was also used a source of music.

Ravenscroft's collection was an important source of home entertainment. While the monophonic psalm tunes were used for liturgical purposes, the harmonizations were used at home. Samuel Sewell (1652-1730), precenter of Boston's Old South Church from 1694 to 1713, recalled singing practices outside the church: "We were Fellows together at College and have sung many a tune in Consort [in parts]."[22] In a second entry Sewell remembered, "In the new Room with the Widow Calis and her daughter Sparhawk; sung the 114th Psalm. Simon catch'd us a base."[23]

The Puritans would have been pleased to use the original music of David had it been preserved; but this was not the case. As has already been established, the elements of musical style were subservient to the words of the psalms and were developed with the same gravity as other elements of Puritan society. In Henry Ainsworth's terms:

> Tunes for the Psalms I find none set of God; so that each people is to use the most grave, decent and comfortable manner of singing that they know. . . . The singing-notes, therefore, I have most taken from our former Englished Psalms, when they will fit the measure of the verse. And for the other long verses I have also taken (for the most part) the gravest and easiest tunes of the French and Dutch psalms.[24]

By the 1630s the Massachusetts Bay Colony had reached as far as New Haven and Hartford. Puritan leaders began to evaluate certain aspects of their society. Many of the more educated Puritans were dissatisfied with the Sternhold and Hopkins psalter. As Robert Stevenson reports, the Pilgrims also "rejected the excessively long tunes, the multiplicity of metrical patterns, the extensive borrowings from continental sources and the jaunty rhythms" found in the Ainsworth psalter.[25] To meet the needs of the colonists, the first edition of the *Whole Book of Psalmes Faithfully Translated into English Metre* was printed in 1640 on a press brought from England two years earlier.[26]

The *Bay Psalm Book*, as it came to be known, was a more accurate paraphrase than Sternhold and Hopkins, if not as poetic. It simplified a number of elements, most notably the variety of meters used. While Sternhold and Hopkins contained psalms in seventeen different meters, the new *Bay Psalm Book* used only six.[27] The 1700 copies of the first edition were quickly distributed and its popularity was assured. It went through seventy editions in the United States, eighteen editions in England, and twenty-two editions in Scotland.[28] The *Bay Psalm Book* became so well respected that the hard-headed Pilgrim communities eventually dropped the Ainsworth psalter to adopt it. The Salem congregations followed in 1667 and the Plymouth congregation in 1685.[29]

The first eight editions of the *Bay Psalm Book* contained no music. The Ravenscroft collection provided tunes until 1698, when the *Bay Psalm Book* was finally published with music.[30] The thirty-nine tunes included are generally modal, and the melodic lines tend to be angular. The rhythms are based on the proportional system of the European Renaissance.

Church music remained simple, as accorded its "seriousness" and "gravity." In the home, music was performed in parts and occasionally with instruments. The Reverend John Cotton, in his treatise *Singing of Psalms a Gospel Ordinance* (1647), remained consistent with Calvin in his tolerance of musical instruments.[31] As Gilbert Chase said, "Their objection to instrumental music in churches was based on religious grounds; it smacked of the 'ceremonial worship' and 'popery' against which the Puritans stood."[32]

2. Choral Music in New England: Eighteenth and Early Nineteenth Centuries

Many Christian churches had been established in the colonies by the eighteenth century. New music continued to be imported, much of it from Britain; anthems and hymns took their place beside traditional psalters. Some Calvinist churches continued the practice of monophonic metrical psalmody. The Dutch Reformed Church of New York, for example, commissioned Francis Hopkinson to make a new translation of the psalms; this psalter was published in 1767 with traditional psalm tunes. Sacred music in America was performed by congregations and choirs and is therefore considered choral even though some of the music is monophonic.

Choral music in the American colonies was dynamic, with new ideas continually being introduced. The Reverend Thomas Symnes (1678-1725), a Harvard graduate and minister in Bradford, Massachusetts, was the driving force behind one of these new ideas. In response to what he perceived as the deterioration in the quality of congregational singing, he published an essay in 1720 titled "The Reasonableness of Regular Singing." It enumerates reasons for learning to read music rather than singing in the "Usual Way" (by oral tradition). The "Regular Singing" controversy raged for years; urban congregations generally sided with Symnes's position, while rural congregations generally rejected it. The controversy not only marks the beginning of the schism between the proponents of refined hymnody versus the less sophisticated practitioners of the oral tradition but resulted in a proliferation of newly created harmonizations of psalm tunes.[33]

The singing school was the response to the call for better congregational singing. Singing schools became popular in rural areas, because they filled educational as well as social needs. The teachers of these schools were itinerant musicians who went from town to town, holding the schools for anywhere from six weeks to four months.[34] Many diaries of the period attest to the significance of the singing schools as social gathering places. As Elizabeth Fuller of Princeton, Massachusetts wrote in her diary on 21 January 1791, "Pleasant weather. Nathan Perry put our horse into their sleigh and carried me to the singing school and back again. I had a fine ride and a fine evening; they sang a great many Tunes. I sang with them."[35] Caleb Jackson of Rowley, Massachusetts, attended a singing school five times in nineteen days.[36] Other documented references span the social classes from unschooled farmers to future president John Adams. The singing school was truly a democratic institution.

To begin, the singing school master would distribute copies of his or another master's tunebook to the class. Tunebooks became a peculiarly popular American phenomenon as a result of their use in singing-school classes. The books usually contained a theoretical introduction explaining the rules of music and sight-reading. The rules of sight-reading were often based on a variation of Guidonian *solfeggio* using the syllables *fa*, *sol*, *la*, and *mi*. This system of syllables simplified the complexities of the seven-note scale; indeed, singing schools became so associated with it that in the nineteenth-century South this type of singing became known as *fasola* singing. Following the introduction, tunebooks contained a selection of psalms, hymns, and anthems for three or four voices.

The first important native tunebook was James Lyon's *Urania*, published in 1761. Lyon (1725-1794), born in Newark, New Jersey, served as a Presbyterian and Congregationalist clergyman in various places until his death. His earliest known composition was an ode for the commencement service of his own Princeton class of 1759. *Urania* consists primarily of the works of other composers, but it also contains several of Lyon's own compositions. Perhaps the most extraordinary of these is the anthem "Two Celebrated Verses by Sternhold & Hopkins Set to Music" ("The Lord Descended from Above"). It is an extended work that includes some thoughtful compositional techniques. Its most apparent characteristic is its textural variety. As Robert Stevenson points out, it "veers from duet to full chorus, exploits the antiphony of answering voices, includes some vocal flourishes that would tax any singer's virtuosity, and divides into sections to be sung at contrasting speeds."[37]

Lyon also makes good use of word painting. In addition to obvious examples (a descending melody on the word "descended," low *tessitura* on "underneath his feet," high *tessitura* on "sky," and florid figurations for "wings" and "flying"), he combines descending and ascending figures for the word "bow'd." He creates a complex melodic figure for the image of the Lord, which is inverted for the cherubim, and uses thundering 16th notes to evoke the image of the Lord riding on the backs of the cherubim.

Francis Hopkinson (1737-1791) is a competitor with Lyon for the title of the first native-born American composer. A prominent man in public life, he was a lawyer and writer, held a judgeship, was the first Secretary of the Navy, and a signer of the Declaration of Independence. He was also a poet, musician, and composer. Hopkinson's music was based on European models. While known primarily for his songs, he was an active church musician, substituted as a church organist, wrote a guidebook for organists, and translated the Psalms (see above). Hopkinson's rector at Christ's Church in Philadelphia preferred metrical psalms to traditional Anglican chant.[38] Hopkinson composed several of these, including the "23d Psalm," which appears in Lyon's *Urania*. Originally, this psalm tune was written in a manuscript book, *Francis Hopkinson, His Book*,[39] while the words of the psalm are not included in *Urania*, they are found in the Hopkinson manuscript.[40] This copy book also contains "An Anthem from the 114th Psalm," the earliest dated American sacred composition, and the first known to have been written in America with a figured bass.[41]

European, particularly British, influence became a point of great contention in American music during the the latter part of the eighteenth century. This acrimony is strongly felt in William

Billings's apologetic for his method of composition in the introduction to his tunebook *The New England Psalm Singer* (1770):

> Perhaps it may be expected by some, that I should say something concerning the Rules of Composition; to these I answer that Nature is the best Dictator, for all the hard, dry, studied Rules that ever was prescribed, will not enable any person to form an air. . . . It must be Nature, Nature must lay the foundation, Nature must inspire the Thought. . . . For my own Part, as I don't think myself confin'd to any Rules for composition, laid down by any that went before me, neither should I think (were I to pretend to lay down Rules) that any one who came after me were any ways obligated to adhere to them, any further that they should think proper; so in fact, I think it best for every *Composer* to be his own *Carver.*[42]

European hegemony was not welcome in the musical world of Billings. It was this attitude that enabled American choral music to develop its own particular sound.

Billings was a tanner by trade before he became a singing master in Stoughton, Massachusetts. He had several physical disabilities, but these did not prevent his participation in the Revolution; he is known to have been a close friend of Sam Adams (they liked to sing hymns together)[43] and Paul Revere, who engraved the frontispiece to *The New England Psalm Singer.*

As a singing master and composer, Billings is considered one of the most important members of the "New England school." His tunebook, *The Singing Master's Assistant*, deserves recognition as perhaps the most important American musical publication of the eighteenth century.[44] There are several reasons for this: all the music and several of the texts were by Billings himself, more than half of the seventy-one compositions were reprinted by later tunebook compilers, and it was the first tunebook published after the beginning of the Revolution. The book became very popular, going through four editions. It is impossible to find a mint copy and difficult to find one in good condition, lending credence to the conclusion that copies were heavily used by their owners.[45] The best reason for its popularity and its importance in the history of American sacred choral music is the music itself. Much of it is splendidly conceived, beautifully executed, and original in sound. Of the seventy-one numbers, most are hymns and psalm tunes. There are also eight anthems, one set piece, and ten fuging tunes.

"Boston" is a lovely Christmas hymn with a text by Billings himself. It had been published in the *New England Psalm Singer* and is reprinted in this volume with slight alterations that were probably made by Billings himself.[46] The meter is common meter doubled (C.M.D., 8.6.8.6.8.6.8.6.) and the form is ABB. Its European Renaissance roots are shown through its homophonic texture, the fact that the melody is in the tenor, and the characteristic rhythmic opening, a half note followed by two quarter notes. J. Murray Barbour likens the piece to a bourée.[47] The melody is folklike,[48] with a strong sense of cadence and key (B-flat). The music, when convincingly performed, is sprightly, tuneful, and very satisfying.[49]

"Jargon" is a satirical study in dissonance, an answer to the critics of his first publication, who claimed that his use of musical materials, especially dissonance, was unschooled (true), and therefore wrong (false). Like most of his compositions "Jargon" is in four parts. It employs some of the same techniques mentioned above, along with several other notable elements: the dynamic markings, which Billings generally ignored, are *forte* and *fortissimo*; the meter is unusual (8.7.8.7.); and original rhythmic augmentations and diminutions are used, giving the piece a plastic quality that expresses the text very effectively. The most striking element of the work, however, is its radical harmonic scheme. After the consonant opening chord, the rest of the composition proceeds with an unbroken series of dissonances, primarily exploiting fourths, sevenths, and ninths. The sound is something closer to Bartok or Copland than to an eighteenth-century composer. That this was meant as a joke should not undermine Billings's genius; no other eighteenth-century musical joke, even that of Mozart's, is at the same time so radical and so interesting. Even the choral writing and voice leading is well done. As Barbour points out:

> It is the great tunefulness of all of Billings voice parts that elevates him above the rest of the composers studied. This is even true of the waggish "Jargon." . . . Of its thirty chords, only the first is consonant; the others fairly bristle with seconds, sevenths, and

> ninths--pandiatonicism a century and a half before Slonimsky! And yet, except for some angularity in the tenor's second phrase, the parts remain wholly singable.[50]

"Chester" is an example of the American tendency to blur the distinctions between the sacred and the secular, a theme that manifests itself not only in America's music but in virtually all aspects of its culture and society. From the time the Puritans came to build the "New Jerusalem," the "City on the Hill," to modern times, when the chaplains of Congress continue to open with a prayer, Americans have tended to believe that God is on their side. Billings used a sacred form, the hymn tune, and poured in patriotic, revolutionary fervor:

> Let tyrants shake their iron rod,
> And Slav'ry clank her galling chains,
> We fear them not, we trust in God,
> New England's God for ever reigns.

Billings's "The Rose of Sharon" is included in the *Singing Master's Assistant* and in numerous other tunebooks such as the highly popular *Missouri Harmony* (discussed in the section on shape note and gospel singing that follows).

The number of composers of choral music increased and hundreds of new works were added to the native repertory at the end of the eighteenth century and the beginning of the nineteenth century. The battle between "right" and "wrong" compositional idioms also intensified. Native composition increased, only to be derided by Europeans and European-influenced Americans. Composers such as Justin Morgan (1747-1798) and Jeremiah Ingalls (1764-1828), not to mention Billings himself, were gradually dropped from northern tunebook collections in favor of more European-influenced composers such as Andrew Law (1748-1821), Thomas Hastings (1784-1872), and Lowell Mason (1792-1872).

Justin Morgan, while not prolific (only nine compositions are extant), wrote music that is highly original and expressive, representative of the native school of American composition. An apparent theme in his music is that of death, and the musical character of the works that deal with that subject directly are reminiscent of the late Renaissance Italian mannerists. Morgan's longest composition is his only anthem, "Judgment Anthem." The text is a composite of two works, an Isaac Watts poem called "The Day of Judgment" and an American hymn entitled "Hark, Ye Mortals," which may have been written by the Reverend Samson Occan, an ordained Presbyterian clergyman who was a Mohican Indian. "Hark, Ye Mortals" first appeared in his *Choice Collection of Hymns and Spiritual Songs*, published in 1774.[51] "Judgment Anthem" uses many startling techniques as expressive means. Changes of texture, *tessitura*, and key (mainly between major and minor mode) abound. Morgan also associates voice parts with subjects in the text. According to Betty Bandel,

> Morgan also seems to have chosen voices to introduce solo passages with special care that the voice should be appropriate to the words being sung. Thus the counter (alto), which was normally sung by boys' voices in Morgan's day, introduces most passages that deal with "Christ victorious," and the high treble (women's voices) sounds the trumpet-like warning of an impending judgment that will lead both to heaven and to hell. In effect, the message of the text was so important to Morgan that he allowed it to dictate the musical form of his composition.[52]

His "Tribulation" and "Amanda" were extremely popular in the singing schools. They are included in *The Missouri Harmony* and were reprinted in several other tunebooks.

Charles Hamm fully discusses the reform movement, which began around the turn of the century, in his *Music in the New World*. Hamm concludes that Lowell Mason's and his fellow reformer's "criticisms of the 'old ways' were more often of the *manner* of singing--vocal production, ornamentation, pitch, the changing of written notes, by individual singers--than of the repertory which was dying anyway."[53] While this statement is basically true, some further explanation is required. The repertory was not really dying, but merely moving westward and southward toward what was to become known as the sacred harp tradition. It was not only the manner of singing that concerned the reformers. Mason demonstrates that with his insistence on European harmonic models in such hymns as "Olivet" and the "Missionary Hymn." Thomas Hastings shows his concern with European forms in his "Ordination Anthem" and his "Dedication." (It is significant that both use figured bass.)

3. Shape-Note and Gospel Hymns in the Midwest and South

The roots of shape-note and gospel music lie in New England, where the reform movement instituted by Lowell Mason and his devotees alienated large numbers of churchgoers and clergy, not to mention some American composers of sacred music. Compilers of tunebooks replaced music by American composers with European or "correct" American works in each succeeding edition of their "end-openers" or "long-boys" as the books were called. As the reformers gained ground in their efforts to purify the country's music, the older American hymns and anthems became entrenched in the rural churches, where they remain to this day. This outcast music was perfectly suited to the defiant fundamentalism that characterized rural religion. Gospel music would later develop from this music, drawing from it many stylistic elements, such as rhythmic excitement and a direct textual expression.

Between 1798 and 1831 several editions of a new kind of tunebook were issued. *The Easy Instructor*, compiled by William Little and William Smith, was designed to make sight-reading of the *fasola* even simpler. (The introductory text of the book is included in this volume.) As John Playford wrote more than a century before *The Easy Instructor* was first published, the four syllables (*fa*, *sol*, *la*, and *mi*) are "sufficient for expressing the several sounds, and less burthensome for the memories of the Practioners."[54] *The Easy Instructor*'s compilers gave the noteheads of each of the four pitches a unique shape, thus making it unnecessary for the singing-school master to teach students the art of reading traditional notation. Irving Lowens credits the edition compiled by Little and Smith as being the first shape-note tunebook in the United States.[55]

The idea was extraordinarily successful, as evidenced by the virtual explosion of nineteenth-century shape-note tunebooks. The shape-note idea was bound to the "native" repertory of Billings and his school and rejected by the reform movement, represented by Andrew Law, Thomas Hastings (who called shape-notes "dunce-notes"[56]), Lowell Mason, William Bradbury, and all those preferring European models of music and singing technique. Shape-note tunebooks thus became wedded to the fundamentalist tradition.

Although Andrew Law was an integral part of the pro-European reform movement, he did invent his own shape-note technique without staff lines. Law initiated and was defeated in a lawsuit against Little and Smith in which he claimed to be the inventor of the shape-note system.[57] "Old 100" and "Delaware" from Law's *Art of Singing* demonstrte his staffless shape-note technique.

The reform movement and its advocates essentially pushed the native repertory, in its new format of shape-notes, toward the geographical areas of least resistance, the South and Midwest. The shape-note tradition (or sacred harp, as it is known today, the term coming from a publication of that title) is one of the few early American musical traditions that still survives. Many hymnbooks are still in print, and in rural parts of the South one can still attend sacred harp sings that bring to life such music as it sounded in Billings's time. The style of music is part of a tradition stretching back to the eighteenth century. In Charles Seeger's words,

> These collections present a distinctive style of choral composition. It is not, in any orthodox sense, a harmonic style. The tones sung by the various voices upon any given beat are not conceived of as being fundamentally a unit--a chord. Instead, each voice added to the tune is related to it independently of the relation between the tune and the other added voice. Thus these pieces may be said to show a definitely contrapuntal style.[58]

The most popular tunebook in the Midwest was Allen D. Carden's *The Missouri Harmony*. It is a typical tunebook, compiled, in Carden's words, "to supply the churches with a competent number of slow and solemn tunes, in unison with the spirit and design of worship."[59] The introductory pages provide an explanation of the gamut: intervals and harmony, key signatures, rhythm and musical notation. This is followed by a selection of hymn tunes and anthems by "the most approved authors"; these include Billings's "The Rose of Sharon," Morgan's "Judgment Anthem," and "Amanda" (all included in *Choral Music in New England: Eighteenth and Early Nineteenth Centuries*), Timothy Swan's "China," and Jeremiah Ingalls's "Northfield."

Little is known about Carden's life. He lived in Nashville, Tennessee, and the surrounding area for most of his life but, because of his singing school activities, traveled widely. *The Missouri Harmony*, one of three tunebooks he compiled, was published in Cincinnati by Morgan and Sanxay. The advertisement for the book and the beginning of a singing school in St. Louis appeared in *The Missouri Gazette and Public Advertiser* on 31 May 1820.[60] The tunebook enjoyed both fame and a considerable amount of popularity.[61] Carl Sandburg mentions its impact on the pioneers of the West in his book *The American Songbag*: "A famous oblong song book of the pioneer days in the middle west was 'Missouri Harmony,' . . . Young Abraham Lincoln and his sweetheart, Ann Rutledge, sang from this book in the Rutledge tavern in New Salem according to old settlers there."[62]

Shape-note tunebooks and sacred harp singing have also gained a recent following in the scholarly community. Music historians, theorists, and ethnomusicologists have published several fine studies of the music,[63] and vocal groups are recording performances.[64] As noted above, publishers have reprinted some of the original books, including *The Sacred Harp, The Social Harp, The Southern Harmony,* and *The New Harp of Columbia*. These shape-note tunebooks also contain gospel humns and music used at camp meetings. Urban hymns from the fundamentalist repertory were eventually added to some of the books.

Religious revivals swept the United States in the late eighteenth and early to mid-nineteenth centuries. Collectively known at the Great Awakening, these revivals were evangelical in character and biblically fundamental in theology. Evangelical rallies were often held outdoors in large tents. These camp meetings inspired a new type of music, another native form also most popular in the south and Midwest: the gospel hymn. The musical style of the gospel hymn was well suited to its evangelical purpose. The music was, to quote Charles Hamm, "written in the most familiar style of the day and repetitions in nature so as to become quickly familiar. The harmonic style is fully triadic, usually drawing on only three or four chords; texts are concerned with sin and salvation; structures resemble those of popular songs of the day with several verses each followed by a chorus or refrain line."[65]

Perhaps the most representative gospel hymn composer was Ira D. Sankey (1840-1908), the musical half of Dwight L. Moody's evangelistic team. Sankey's songs (and others) were published between 1875 and 1891 as gospel hymns and sacred songs. A representative example of Sankey's work is seen in "A Soldier of the Cross," hymn no. 494 of his 1894 publication *Gospel Hymns Nos. 1-6 Complete*.

Women were not excluded from gospel hymn writing. One of the most popular songs of all times, "Blessed Assurance,"[66] was a collaborative effort between lyricist Fanny Crosby and composer Phoebe Knapp (1839-1908). Knapp is one of the few women to be included in Sankey's *Gospel Hymns* ("Blessed Assurance" is no. 304), and she holds a significant place in the history of American music general as well as in the history of church music. "She represents a new type of composer that appeared in the 1860's--the woman who was not primarily interested in household music or accomplishment, but came to music through another path. Phoebe Knapp's parents were famous leaders in the Perfectionist Revivals of the 1840's and 50's, and her mother, Phoebe Palmer, was a hymnist and the author of several well-known religious treatises."[67] Her music is on a par with Sankey's; often her harmonic vocabulary is more adventuresome than that of the usual gospel hymn.[68]

4. African-American Music

African-American music poses particular problems to the anthologizer, but its importance to American musical history demands representation. Given that only the published approximations of the oral tradition are available, a historical anthology cannot adequately communicate the richness of the black musical tradition. While it is not impossible to trace the African-American musical heritage,[69] it is difficult to find adequate written examples of black music. As

Eileen Southern writes, "The white settlers brought their psalm books to the new world and later imported musical instruments. The black folk brought their memories of the rich traditions of Africa. Together the settlers, black and white, were to lay the foundation for a phenomenal subsequent development of music in America."[70]

Because the black contribution to early American music is primarily oral, its history has often been misunderstood, as in the example of the spiritual. George Pullen Jackson in *White Spirituals in the Southern Uplands* and Richard Wallaschek in *Primitive Music* both maintain that the black spiritual was completely derived from white hymns.[71] Dena Epstein rightfully debunks their historigraphical methodologies, pointing out that "parallels between white and black spirituals certainly exist, but they must be considered together with other kinds of evidence, stylistic, historical, iconographic, and ethnomusicological from Europe, Africa, and the Americas to reach valid conclusions. Any theory about folk music that ignores the sound of the music and how it is performed cannot be valid."[72] This is an especially apt conclusion considering that the written music used in the white and black churches was identical. Southern writes: "until after the American Revolution, black Protestants worshipped alongside whites in the meeting houses of colonial America (albeit in segregated pews) and sang the standard Protestant psalms and hymns."[73]

The sound of early black singing was influenced by African musical practices. As early as 1693 African Americans organized their own meetings after the Sabbath evening services, in which they sang psalms away from the restrictions of whites.[74] By the 1770s, when blacks began splitting from white congregations, a style of African-American choral singing had been born and was thriving. A Russian observer, Paul Svin'in described the singing at Bethel Chapel, Philadelphia, in 1811:

> At the end of every psalm the entire congregation, men and women alike, sang verses in a loud, shrill monotone. This lasted about half an hour. When the preacher ceased reading, all turned toward the door, fell on their knees, bowed their heads to the ground and set up an agonizing, heart-rending moaning. Afterwards, the minister resumed the reading of the psalter and when he had finished sat down on a chair; then all rose and began

> chanting psalms in chorus, the men and women alternating, a procedure which lasted some twenty minutes.[75]

As Southern notes, the call-and-response and antiphonal methods as well as intense emotionalism are typical of African musical idioms. It is encouraging that scholars are beginning to address the issue of source and sound. In an article published in 1982, Brett Sutton studied the relationship between published tune-books since 1800 and the hymnody of the rural South that survives in the oral tradition.[76] By comparing the ways identical hymns are sung in white and black churches and comparing these performance styles with the written sources of the hymns, Sutton has convincingly shown why historians cannot rely on written sources alone.

There are certain inflections, turns of phrase, and alterations of pitch common in the performance of music in black churches that are not indicated in the written music. Rhythmic alterations also occur. It is impossible to accurately depict what is actually taking place during the singing of African-American music because written symbols for it do not exist in the standard European system of music notation. In contrast, singing in white churces tends to follow the written notation literally.

Another problem facing the anthologizer is the loss of written sources once known to exist. One of the earliest black music teachers and singing-school masters was Newport Gardner (1746-1826). A slave who bought his freedom with the winnings from a lottery, he started his own singing school in 1791 after studying with Andrew Law. He was the composer of several works, including a choral composition called "Promise Anthem"; unfortunately, no copy is known to exist.[77]

A third problem arises when the music is not included in the hymnal. In 1801 Richard Allen (1760-1831), an influential black Methodist minister, compiled *A Collection of Spiritual Songs and Hymns Selected from Various Authors*, the first hymnal designed exclusively for the needs of an all-black congregation. Allen was not a composer, however, and the hymns were sung to commonly used tunes, none of which were included in the hymnal.

It was not until after the Civil War, when African Americans began their arduous journey of integration into American society, that their music was disseminated. The first large collection of spirituals was *Slave Songs of the United States*, published in 1867. ("The Good Old Way," "I'm Going Home," "Sinner Won't Die No More," and "These Are All My Father's Children" are included here.) This collection contains both the words and music to songs. The transcriptions are monophonic and are written out in traditional western notation, without the diacritical markings so common in modern ethnomusicological transcription. William Francis Allen, one of the compilers of *Slave Songs*, points out the difficulty of transcribing the spirituals into traditional western notation: "The best that we can do, however, with paper and types, or even with voices, will convey, but a faint shadow of the original. The voices of the colored people have a peculiar quality that nothing can imitate; and the intonations and delicate variations of even one singer cannot be reproduced on paper."[78] Luckily, Allen does provide detailed information on the performance style in his introduction.[79]

The Fisk Jubilee Singers were also important contributors to the dissemination of black choral music. Fisk University in Nashville, Tennessee, opened its doors in 1866 with a commitment to provide recently freed young slaves with a university education. George White, a white instructor, devoted his free time to music instruction. White formed the Fisk Jubilee Singers, who gave their first concert in 1867. By 1871 they were touring, singing both spirituals and popular songs. White was very careful to avoid having his group identified with blackface minstrel show performers; the Fisk Jubilee Singers eventually won great acclaim. The songs included from the Jubilee Singers repertory come from two sources, *The Story of the Jubilee Singers* by J. B. T. Marsh ("Ride on, King Jesus," "What Kind of Shoes Are You Going to Wear?" "Inching Along," and "I Ain't Got Weary Yet") and *Jubilee and Plantation Songs,* which is a later attempt to adapt the spiritual to Western musical notation ("O Sinner, You'd Better Get Ready" and "Rise and Shine").

The spiritual was not the black American's only contribution to choral repertory. In 1881 a Boston postal employee named James Monroe Trotter published an extraordinary book, *Music and Some Highly Musical People*, a survey of black contributions to American music.[80] As Robert Stevenson points out, Trotter's book preceded Frederic Louis Ritter's *Music in America* (1883, considered the first history of American music) by several years and "ought to be hailed as a first of its kind black or white." Stevenson continues:

> No previous historian had transcended New England, no previous author had taken account of both sacred and secular outpourings, no previous chronicler had documented his running narrative with a 152-page musical appendix containing thirteen vocal and instrumental selections (mostly complete) by twelve different composers. How distinctive was Trotter's appendix (a luxury not duplicated in any later American music history to date) becomes all the more apparent when the geographical and age spread of the twelve composers is considered: Boston, New York, Cleveland and New Orleans being represented impartially, and the composers in the appendix ranging from a mere eighteen-year old Bostonian to a veteran New Yorker who had died in 1854.[81]

One of the two choral compositions presented in Trotter's appendix is a Mass for Three Voices, by the New Orleans musician and composer Samuel Snaer (ca. 1832-after 1880). He was evidently a highly regarded performer (piano, violin, cello) as well as a music teacher and organist at St. Mary's Catholic Church in New Orleans.[82] Trotter evinces great respect for Snaer, calling him a "brilliant pianist" and a "ready composer."[83] As Trotter reports, however, his music was not widely circulated because

> extreme modesty . . . has prevented him from publishing many of his pieces. Generally his habit has been to sit down and compose a piece, and then allow the manuscript to go the rounds among his acquaintances. As he would make no request for its return, nor express solicitude regarding its fate, the music rarely returned to the composer; so that to-day the most unlikely place to find copies of his work is at the professor's own residence.[84]

The "Gloria" from Snaer's Mass demonstrates his fine technique. Scored for three male voices (two tenors and bass) and orchestra (as evidenced from the trumpet indication of the piano reduction), the work is written in the idiom of the early romantic period. The harmonic language is similar to Mendelssohn's; the rhythmic writing is lively and full of energy. Snaer shows his personal voice in the melodic writing with ideas that are fresh and at times unusual.

5. The Nineteenth-Century Classical Tradition

While Billings and his compatriots were active during the latter half of the eighteenth century, America was receiving a steady stream of European musicians and composers who wished to establish themselves in the new country. These emigres directly influenced the reform movement in American psalmody and contributed to the development of an American tradition of classical composition. Five large works, either excerpted or complete, have been chosen to represent this tradition here. All have music of interest, and none are easily available elsewhere.

Charles Zeuner (1795-1857), an archetypical romantic in life and death, emigrated from Eisleben, Germany, around 1830,[85] already an established composer. He settled first in Boston, then in Philadelphia, where he earned his living as a church organist. He held the presidency of Boston's Handel and Haydn Society, 1838-39, a period when he was expected to serve as the director of the society's chorus. But "his temper was such that he could not keep harmony among the singers and he resigned when requested to do so."[86]

The *Fall of Zion,* his solo cantata for bass voice and small orchestra, is not mentioned by Zeuner's biographers but it is a microcosm of his style. Oliver Strunk summarizes this style as follows: "Employing the conventional German style of the 1820s, his more serious compositions . . . are at least fluent and pleasing, show real skill in handling orchestral and choral masses, and have occasional moments of real dignity."[87] *The Fall of Zion* fits most of these characteristics, in addition to showing a dramatic flare in the solo line and an overall Sturm und Drang that is rare in the church music of Zeuner's contemporaries. Indeed, it would probably be well-received if it were performed today. The text by E. Taylor is a paraphrase of words from the Book of Jeremiah.

Although there is no record of Charles Zeuner's having been a member of the Musical Fund Society of Philadelphia (founded 1820), it was in the library of this organization that the manuscript score was found. Sam Dennison found the score in 1974, while cataloging the Musical Fund Society's holdings. He subsequently prepared the edition found here. There is no date on the score, nor is there evidence that the work was ever performed, since no parts have been located. The manuscript score does show some wear, however, and markings that indicate that some rehearsing was done, perhaps in preparation for a performance that failed to take place.

John Knowles Paine (1839-1906), a professor of music at Harvard from 1873 until his death, was distinguished in being, in the words of Charles Hamm, "the first American composer to write major works in the Germanic style fully comparable in quality to the products of European writers."[88] One of his most impressive works was the oratorio *St. Peter* (1872), perhaps the first oratorio written on American soil by a native composer. An excellent account of its performance history and an analysis of the various sections can be found in John C. Schmidt's study of the composer's life and works.[89] An orchestral score of *St. Peter* edited by Gunther Schuller is now available from GunMar Music, and it has been recorded on GM Recordings (GM 2027CD-2).

The 1876 Centennial of the Declaration of Independence should have been an excellent showcase for America's musical talents. But Americans, still not convinced of the talents of their own native composers,[90] were not to be contented with an all-American musical program. The ceremonies highlighted a work commissioned from Richard Wagner for a king's ransom of $5,000 as well as Handel's "Dettingen" *Te Deum.*[91] Compared with the efforts of the Americans, Wagner's work was judged the weakest; indeed, even Wagner belittled it: "Do you know what is the best thing about the March?" he asked. "The money I got for it."[92]

Programmed alongside Wagner's march was John Knowles Paines' *Centennial Hymn* and Dudley Buck's *The Centennial Meditation of Columbia*. Buck (1839-1909) was trained in Paris and Leipzig[93] and his style demonstrates a mastery of German Romantic musical idioms. His *Centennial Meditation of Columbia*, a large-scale cantata with a text by Sidney Lanier, was very well received by several rather hard-boiled critics. William Apthorp, while criticizing Lanier's poetry, said that Buck "never allows the dramatic possibilities of his text to lure him away from a musically self-dependent and consistent form," evidently very high praise from Apthorp.[94]

William Wallace Gilchrist (1846-1916) was a composer and organist/choirmaster active in both Cincinnati and Philadelphia. He was the founder and conductor (for forty years) of Philadelphia's Mendelssohn Club and was the editor of the Presbyterian Church's official hymnal (*The Hymnal*, 1895). Robert Stevenson ranks him "among the most successful serious American composers of his generation."[95] Gilchrist's *46th Psalm* won the Cincinnati May Festival Prize ($1000) in 1882, in a competition judged by Saint-Saëns, Reinecke, and Theodore Thomas.[96] Martha Furman Schleifer describes the style of the psalm: "Gilchrist uses motivic development in this work for orchestra, full chorus, and soprano solo. In a dramatic, effective treatment of the psalm, he freely uses assorted musical textures, word-painting and modulation to reflect mood changes. The final large division of the four-section work includes a fugue, the subject introduced by bass voices which is combined with a 'gloria patri' to create a powerful climactic end."[97]

This anthology concludes with an excerpt from an impressive work by Amy Marcy Cheney (Mrs. H. H. A.) Beach (1867-1944). Beach has historically been associated with the so-called Boston, or second New England, school (which included Horatio Parker, George Whitefield Chadwick, and Arthur Foote), though she did not attend their meetings. Beach came from a musical home and quickly established herself as a child prodigy. By the age of seven she appeared as a pianist playing her own compositions, and at sixteen she made her professional debut in a performance of the G-minor concerto of Moscheles.

Beach had only one year of formal training in harmony and was essentially self-taught as a composer; she learned orchestration by translating Berlioz's treatise on orchestration. This lack of formal training in no way hindered her prolific compositional life. While best known for her songs and chamber music, she was, in the words of Adrienne Fried Block, "a highly disciplined composer, capable of producing large scale works in a few days."[98] This mastery of large forms is well demonstrated by the "Kyrie" and "Gloria" movements of her *Mass in E flat,* published in 1890 when she was only twenty-three.

The "Kyrie" is scored for organ, strings, winds, and horns in pairs, and the "Gloria" adds trombones, trumpets, and tympani. While the orchestration is obviously based on German models and is essentially conservative, the formal procedures are more original. Motivic repetitions are employed at important structural points, and there is a gradual unfolding of thematic materials rather than an overly structured form, indicating French influences. The "Gloria" demonstrates a powerful flair for drama, and both movements show the great melodic expressiveness and control of modulatory techniques that define Beach's compositional voice.

Philip Vandermeer
VOLUME EDITOR

Notes

1. Quoted in David McKay, "Cotton Mather's Unpublished Singing Sermon," *New England Quarterly* 48, no. 3 (September 1975): 416.

2. Quoted in John Stevens, *Music and Poetry in the Early Tudor Court* (New York: Cambridge University Press, 1961, 1979), 81.

3. Albert Dunning, "Calvin [Cauvin], Jean," in *The New Grove Dictionary of Music and Musicians,* vol. 3 (New York: Macmillan, 1980), 630.

4. Quoted in John Calvin, *Institutes of the Christian Religion,* 2 vols., ed. John T. McNeill, trans. Ford Lewis Battles (Philadelphia: Westminster Press, 1960), book IV, ch. XX, no. 32, 895f. Calvin also quotes two other scripture passages: "I will sing with the spirit and I will sing with the mind" (I Corinthians 14:15) and "Teaching one another . . . in hymns, psalms, and spiritual songs, singing with thankfulness in your hearts to the Lord" (Colossians 3:16f).

5. Calvin, *Institutes*, book IV, ch. XX, no. 31, 894.

6. John Calvin, *Genesis*, trans. and ed. John King (Edinburgh: Banner of Truth Trust, 1965), 218.

7. Calvin, *Institutes*, book IV, ch XX, no. 32, 895-96.

8. Ibid., 896, [no. 1].

9. Nicholas Temperley, Howard Slenk, Margaret Munck, and John M. Barkley, "Psalmody (ii)" *New Grove Dictionary*, vol. 15, 347.

10. Gustave Reese, *Music in the Renaissance*, rev. ed. (New York: Norton, 1954, 1959), 359. Reese reports the psalter contains eighteen psalm settings (six by Calvin, twelve by Marot] and three canticles [all by Calvin]. The *New Grove* reports a total of nineteen psalm settings.

11. Temperley et al, "Psalmody (ii)," 348.

12. Ibid., 349.

13. Richard Terry, ed., *Calvin's First Psalter* [1539] (London: Ernest Benn, 1932).

14. Several good treatments of the subject include Nicholas Temperly, *The Music of the English Parish Church*, 2 vols. (New York: Cambridge University Press, 1979), and Temperly et al, "Psalmody (ii)," 337-82.

15. As Samuel Eliot Morison reports in his introduction to William Bradford's *Of Plymouth Plantation: 1620-1647* (New York: Knopf, 1963), xi: "About 100 persons reached Plymouth in the *Mayflower* in December 1620. Ten years later, after new arrivals by the *Anne*, the *Rotune*, the *Little James* and the *Talbot*, the total population was about 300. In 1650, when Governor Bradford stopped writing, there were less than a thousand people under his jurisdiction."

16. For a biographical sketch of Ainsworth, see Waldo Seldon Pratt, *The Music of the Pilgrims* (Boston: Oliver Ditson, 1921), 7-8. There are references to the Pilgrims using Ainsworth's Old Testament commentaries in Bradford, *Plymouth Plantation*, 113, 410.

17. Pratt, *Music of the Pilgrims*, 8.

18. Gilbert Chase, *America's Music, From the Pilgrims to the Present* (New York: McGraw-Hill, 1955), 17.

19. Oscar T. Barck and Hugh T. Lefler, *Colonial America*, 2d ed. (New York: Macmillan, 1968), 85.

20. Charles Hamm, *Music in the New World* (New York: Norton: 1983), 27.

21. Ibid., 27-28.

22. Samuel Sewell, *The Diary of Samuel Sewell, 1674-1729*, 2 vols. (New York: Farrar, Straus and Giroux, 1973). Sewell's diary is liberally sprinkled with references to psalm singing in parts as a social activity.

23. Ibid., 394.

24. From the introduction to the Ainsworth *Psalter*; quoted in Pratt, *Music of the Pilgrims*, 13.

25. Robert Stevenson, *Protestant Church Music in America* (New York: Norton, 1966), 13.

26. Hamm, *Music in the New World*, 28.

27. Irving Lowens, *Music and Musicians in Early America* (New York: Norton, 1964), 32. The edition produced in 1651 used only five meters.

28. Hamm, *Music in the New World*, 29; Temperley, in his *Music of the English Parish Church*, vol 1, 80, points out that the English Puritans used the evidence of the *Bay Psalm Book* as a precedent for their own criticism and reform of Sternhold and Hopkins: "The Sternhold and Hopkins version of the psalms had long been under attack, especially in Calvinist circles, for its departures from strictly literal translation of the Hebrew texts. . . . Now, with the ascendancy of the Long Parliament, such an opportunity seemed to be at hand; and for encouragement there was the recent example of the 'Bay psalm book,' printed at Cambridge, Massachusetts, in 1640 (Cotton, et al.). William Barton was invited to prepare a revised translation, which he brought out in 1644."

29. Stevenson, *Protestant Church Music in America*, 14.

30. Richard G. Appel, *The Music of the Bay Psalm Book, 9th Edition (1698)*, I.S.A.M. Monographs, no. 5. (New York: Institute for Studies in American Music, 1975), v.

31. John Cotton, *Singing of Psalmes a Gospel Ordinance. Or a Treatise wherein Are Handled These Foure Particulars. I. Touching the Duty Itselfe. II. Touching the Matter to Be Sung. III. Touching the Singers. IIII. Touching the Manner of Singing* (London: printed by M. S. for H. Allen and J. Rothwell, 1647). Extant copies may be found at both the New York and Boston Public Libraries.

32. Chase, *America's Music,* 9.

33. Hamm, *Music in the New World*, 41.

34. Edith Boroff, *Music in Europe and the United States: A History* (Englewood Cliffs, N.J.: Prentice- Hall, 1971), 417.

35. Alan Buechner, *Notes to "The New England Harmony"* (New York: Folkways Records), Album no. FA2377, 1964.

36. Ibid.

37. Stevenson, *Protestant Church Music in America*, 50.

38. Robert Stevenson, "The Music that George Washington Knew: Neglected Phrases." *Inter-American Music Review* 5 (Fall 1982): 63.

39. *Francis Hopkinson, His Book,* is a 206-page autograph in the collection of the Library of Congress.

40. Words of the 23d Psalm:

> The Lord himself the mighty Lord
> Vouchsafes to be my Guide
> Vouchsafes to be my Guide
> The Shepherd by whose tender Care
> my Wants are all supplied
> my Wants are all supplied.

41. Stevenson, "The Music that George Washington Knew," 77.

42. William Billings, *The New England Psalm Singer* (Boston: printed by Edes and Gill, 1770).

43. Frank J. Metcalf, *American Writers and Compilers of Sacred Music* (New York: Abingdon Press, 1925), 55.

44. David McKay and Richard Crawford, *William Billings of Boston: Eighteenth-Century Composer* (New Jersey: Princeton University Press, 1975), 77. This book includes detailed studies of Billings's tunebooks, including *The Singing Master's Assistant.*

45. Ibid., 78-79. This is well demonstrated by the copy at the Free Library of Philadelphia. Several pages are missing, including the outrageous (and, apparently to its owner, offensive) "Jargon."

46. Stevenson, *Protestant Church Music in America*, 62.

47. J. Murray Barbour, *The Church Music of William Billings* (East Lansing: Michigan State University Press, 1960), 44-45.

48. Stevenson, *Protestant Church Music in America*, 62.

49. A good recording is the Western Wind vocal sextet *Christmas in the New World* (Musical Heritage Society, MHS 4077), side 1, band 3.

50. Barbour, *Church Music of William Billings*, 99.

51. Betty Bandel, *Sing the Lord's Song in a Strange Land: The Life of Justin Morgan* (Rutherford, N.J.: Fairleigh Dickinson University Press, 1981), 205.

52. Ibid.

53. Charles Hamm, *Music in the New World* (New York: Norton), 171. See pp. 159-72 for Hamm's discussion of the reform movement.

54. John Playford, *An Introduction to the Skill of Musick* (London: printed by W. Goodbid for J. Playford, 1674; reprint, Ridgewood, N.J.: Gregg Press, 1966), 1-2.

55. Irving Lowens, "*The Easy Instructor* (1798-1831: A History and Bibliography of the First Shape-Note Tune-Book," *Music and Musicians in Early America* (New York: Norton, 1964) 117-18.

56. Ibid., 118.

57. Ibid., 58-88.

58. Charles Seeger, "Contrapuntal Style in the Three-Voice Shape-Note Hymns of the United States," in *Studies in Musicology, 1935-1975* (Berkeley: University of California Press, 1977), 237-51.

59. Allen D. Carden, *The Missouri Harmony* (Cincinnati: Morgan and Sanxay, 1833), 4.

60. David L. Crouse, "Allen D. Carden: Early Tennessee Musician," *Tennessee Historical Quarterly* 39, no. 1 (Spring 1980): 12.

61. Seeger, "Contrapuntal Style," 237.

62. From Carl Sandburg, *The American Songbag* (New York: Harcourt, Brace, and Co., 1927), 152; quoted in Crouse, "Allen D. Carden," 15.

63. In addition to those works cited and the many works by George Pullen Jackson, two studies are of value: Buell E. Cobb, Jr., *The Sacred Harp: A Tradition and Its Music* (Athens: University of Georgia, 1978), and Dorothy D. Horn, *Sing to Me of Heaven: A Study of Folk and Early American Materials in Three Old Harp Books* (Gainesville: University of Florida Press, 1970). The Library of Congress Archives of Folk Song published a bibliography entitled *Shaped-Note Singing: A List of References.*

64. Several excellent recordings of shape-note singing include one by a commercial group, the Word of Mouth Chorus, on a Nonesuch recording called *Rivers of Delight* (H-71360) and a field recording issued by the Library of Congress called *Sacred Harp Singing* (AFS L11).

65. Charles Hamm, *Music in the New World*, 277.

66. Robert Stevenson, *Protestant Church Music in America*, 110, n. 270, reports "Blessed Assurance" to be the most popular hymn in the history of the Billy Graham Crusades.

67. Judith Tick, *American Women Composers before 1870* (Ann Arbor, Mich.: UMI Research Press, 1983), 119.

68. Ibid.

69. Eileen Southern, *The Music of Black Americans: A History*, 2d ed. (New York: Norton, 1983), 25.

70. Ibid., 23.

71. Dena J. Epstein, "A White Origin for the Black Spiritual? An Invalid Theory and How It Grew," *American Music* 1 (Summer 1983), 53. See George Pullen Jackson, *White Spirituals in the Southern Uplands* (Chapel Hill: University of North Carolina Press, 1933) and Richard Wallascheck, *Primitive Music* (London, 1893).

72. Ibid., 58.

73. Eileen Southern, "Musical Practices in Black Churches of Philadelphia and New York, ca. 1800-1844," *Journal of the American Musicological Society* 30 (Summer 1977), 297.

74. Southern, *Music of Black Americans*, 33.

75. Ibid., 79.

76. Brett Sutton, "Shape-Note Tunebooks and Primitive Hymns," *Ethnomusicology* 26 (January 1982): 11-26.

77. Southern, *Music of Black Americans*, 70.

78. William F. Allen, Charles Ware, and Lucy M. Garrison, *Slave Songs of the United States* (New York: Agathynian Press, 1867), iv-v.

79. Ibid., xliii-xliv.

80. James Monroe Trotter, *Music and Some Highly Musical People* (Boston: Lee and Shepard, 1881).

81. Robert Stevenson, "America's First Black Music Historian." *Journal of the American Musicological Society* 26 (Fall 1973): 384-85.

82. Eileen Southern, *Biographical Dictionary of Afro-American and African Musicians* (Westport, Conn.: Greenwood Press, 1982), 351.

83. James M. Trotter, *Music and Some Highly Musical People* (Boston: Lee and Shepard, 1881, 342; reprint, New York: Johnson Reprint Co., 1968).

84. Ibid.

85. Oliver Strunk, "Zeuner, Charles," in *Dictionary of American Biography* (New York: Scribners, 1936), 651-52.

86. Metcalf, *American Writers and Compilers of Sacred Music*, 221.

87. Strunk, "Zeuner, Charles," 652.

88. Hamm, *Music in the New World*, 319.

89. John C. Schmidt, *The Life and Works of John Knowles Paine* (Ann Arbor, Mich.: UMI Research Press, 1980), 423-31.

90. One hundred years later the official commission of the U.S. Bicentennial went to foreign composer Krysztof Penderecki for his opera *Paradise Lost*.

91. Martha Furman Schleifer, in "Centennial Exhibition," *New Grove Dictionary of American Music* (*Amerigrove*), vol. 1, (New York: Macmillan, 1986), 382.

92. Henry T. Finck, *Wagner and His Works,* vol. 2 (New York: Charles Scribner's Sons, 1904), 509.

93. Charles Claghorn, "Dudley Buck," in *Biographical Dictionary of American Music* (West Nyack, N.Y.: Parker, 1973), 72.

94. Quoted in Joseph A. Musselman, *Music in the Cultured Generation: A Social History of Music in America, 1870-1900* (Evanston, Ill.: Northwestern University Press, 1971), 119-20.

95. Robert Stevenson, "Gilchrist, William Wallace," *Amerigrove*, vol. 2, 219.

96. Ibid.

97. Martha Furman Schleifer, *William Wallace Gilchrist (1846-1916): A Moving Force in the Musical Life of Philadelphia* (Metuchen, N.J.: Scarecrow Press, 1985), 55.

98. Adrienne Fried Block, "Beach, Amy Marcy (Cheney), in *Amerigrove*, vol. 1, 164.

AMERICAN SACRED MUSIC

1. Early Psalmody

THE BOOK OF PSALMES

Collected into English Meeter, by THOMAS STERNHOLD, JOHN HOPKINS and others: conferred with the Hebrew, with apt Notes to sing them withall.

Set forth and allowed to be sung in all Churches, of all the people together before and after Morning and Evening Prayer.

As also before and after Sermons, and moreover in private Houses, for their godly solace and comfort, laying apart all ungodly Songs and Ballads, which tend onely to the nourishing of vice, and corrupting of youth.

COLOSSIANS III.

Let the Word of God dwell plenteously in you in all wisedome, teaching and exhorting one another in Psalmes, Hymnes, and spirituall Songs, and sing unto the Lord in your hearts.

JAMES V.

If any be afflicted, let him pray: if any be merry, let him sing Psalmes.

LONDON;

Printed by *M. B.* for the Company of Stationers 1647

Cum Privilegio

17 For why, in number they exceed
the haires upon my head.
My heart doth faint for very dread,
that I am almost dead.
18 With speed send help, and set me free,
O Lord I thee require:
Make haste with ayd to succour me,
O Lord, at my desire.

19 Let them sustaine rebuke and shame
that seeke my soule to spill:
Drive back my foes, and them defame
that wish and would me ill.
20 For their ill feats doe them descry
that would deface my name:
Alwayes at me they raile and cry,
fie on him, fie for shame.

21 Let them in thee have joy and wealth
that seeke to thee alwayes:
That those that love thy saving health
may say, To God be praise.
22 But as for me, I am but poore,
opprest and brought full low:
Yet thou, O Lord, wilt me restore
to health, full well I know.

23 For why? thou art my hope and trust,
my refuge, help, and stay:
Wherefore my God, as thou art just
with me, no time delay.

Beatus qui intelligit. Psal. xlj. T. S.

David grievously afflicted, blesseth them that pity his case, complaining on his faithlesse friends, such as Judas, Joh. 13. *Then he giveth thankes for Gods mercy in chastising him gently, and not suffering his enemies to triumph.*

3 And in his bed when he lyes sick
the Lord will him restore:
And thou O Lord wilt turne to health
his sicknesse and his sore.
4 Then in my sicknesse thus said I,
have mercy Lord on me:
And heale my soule which is full woe,
that I offended thee.

5 Mine enemies wish me ill in heart,
and thus of me did say:
When shall he dye, that all his name
may vanish quite away.
6 And when they come to visit me,
they aske if I doe well:
But in their hearts mischiefe they hatch,
and to their mates it tell.

7 They bite their lips, and whisper so,
as though they would me charme:
And cast their fetches how to trap
me with some mortall harme.
8 Some grievous sin hath brought him to
this sicknesse say they plaine:
He is so low, that without doubt
rise can he not againe.

9 The man also that I did trust,
with me did use deceit:
Who at my table eat my bread,
the same for me laid wait.
10 Have mercy Lord on me therefore,
and let me be preserv'd:
That I may render unto them
the things they have deserv'd.

11 By this I know assuredly
to be belov'd of thee:
When that mine enemies have no cause
to triumph over me.
12 But in my right thou hast me kept,
and maintained alway:
And in thy presence place assign'd
where I shall dwell for aye.

13 The Lord the God of Israel
be praised evermore:
Even so be it, Lord, will I say,
even so be it therefore.

Quemadmodum. Psal. xlij. I. H.

David is grieved, that through persecutors he could not be present in the congregation, protesting his presence in heart, albeit in body separate: at last he sheweth that notwithstanding these sorrowes and thoughts, yet he continually putteth his trust in the Lord.

Like as the Hart doth breath and bray *Sing this as the 15. Psalme.*
the well-springs to obtaine,
So doth my soule desire alway
with thee Lord to remaine.
2 My soule doth thirst, and would draw neare
the living Lord of might:
O when shall I come and appeare
in presence of his sight?

For he hath wrought throughout the world,
his wonders great and strong.
2 With his right hand full worthily,
he doth his foes devoure:
And get himselfe the victory,
with his owne arme and power.

3 The Lord doth make the people know
his saving health and might:
The Lord doth eke his justice show,
in all the heathens sight.
4 His grace and truth to Israel,
in minde he doth record:
That all the earth hath seene right well
the goodnesse of the Lord.

5 Be glad in him with joyfull voyce,
all people on the earth:
Give thankes to God, sing and rejoyce,
to him with joy and mirth.
6 Upon the harpe unto him sing,
give thanks to him with Psalmes:
Rejoyce before the Lord our King,
with trumpets and with shalmes.

7 Yea let the sea with all therein,
for joy both roare and swell:
The earth likewise, let it begin,
with all that therein dwell.
8 And let the flouds rejoyce their fils,
and clap their hands apace,
And eke the mountaines and the hils,
before the Lord his face.

9 For he shall come to judge and try,
the world and every wight:
And rule the people mightily,
with justice and with right.

Dominus regnavit. Psal. XCix. I.H.

He commendeth the power, equity, and excellency of the Kingdome of God by Christ, over the Jewes and Gentiles, provoking them to magnifie the same, and to feare the Lord, as the ancient Fathers, Moses, Aaron, and Samuel, who calling upon God, were heard in their prayers.

THe Lord doth raigne, although at it
the people rage full sore:
Yea, he on Cherubins doth sit,
though all the world doe roare.
2 The Lord that doth in Sion dwell,
is high and wondrous great:
Above all folke he doth excell,
and he aloft is set.

3 Let all men praise thy mighty name,
for it is fearfull sure:
And let them magnifie the same,
that holy is and pure.
4 The princely power of our King,
doth love judgement and right:
Thou rightly rulest every thing,
in Iacob through thy might.

5 To praise the Lord our God devise,
all honour to him doe:
His footstoole worship him before,
for hee is holy too.
6 Moses, Aaron, and Samuel,
as priests on him did call:
When they did pray, he heard them well,
and gave them answer all.

7 Within the cloud to them he spake,
then did they labour still:
To keepe such lawes as he did make,
and pointed them untill.
8 O Lord our God, thou didst them heare,
and answeredst them againe:
Thy mercy did on them appeare,
their deeds didst not maintaine.

9 O laud and praise our God and Lord,
within his holy hill:
For why? our God throughout the world,
is holy ever still.

Iubilate Deo omnis. Psal. C.

Hee exhorteth all men to serve the Lord, who hath made us, to enter into his courts, and assemblies to praise his name.

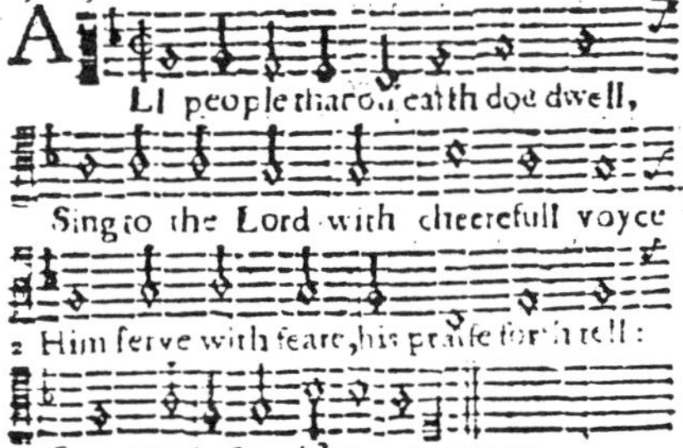

3 The Lord ye know is God indeed,
without our aide he did us make:
We are his flocke, he doth us feed
and for his sheepe he doth us take.
4 O enter then his gates with praise,
approach with joy his courts unto:
Praise, laud, and blesse his name alwayes,
for it is seemely so to doe.

5 For why? the Lord our God is good,
his mercy is for ever sure:
His truth at all times firmely stood,
and shall from age to age endure.

Another of the same.

IN God the Lord be glad and light,
praise him throughout the earth:
Serve him and come before his sight,
with singing and with mirth.

Sing this as the 68 Psalme.

2 Know

THE PSALMS OF DAVID,

WITH

THE TEN COMMANDMENTS, CREED, LORD's PRAYER, &c.

IN METRE.

ALSO,

THE CATECHISM, CONFESSION OF FAITH, LITURGY, &c.

Tranflated from the *DUTCH.*

For the USE of the Reformed Proteftant Dutch Church of the City of NEW-YORK.

NEW-YORK:
Printed by JAMES PARKER, at the New Printing-Office in *Beaver-Street.* MDCCLXVII.

1767

P S A L M LX.

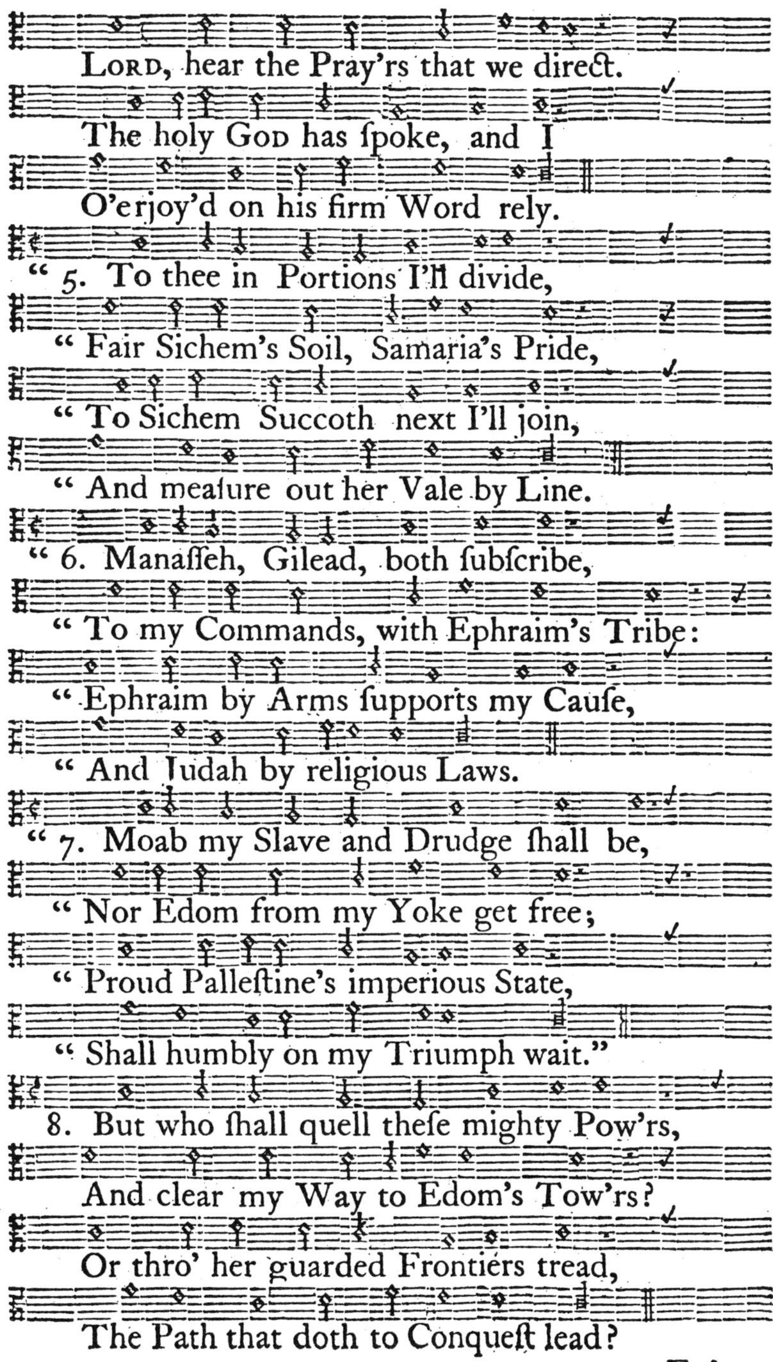

9. Ev'n

PSALM LXI.

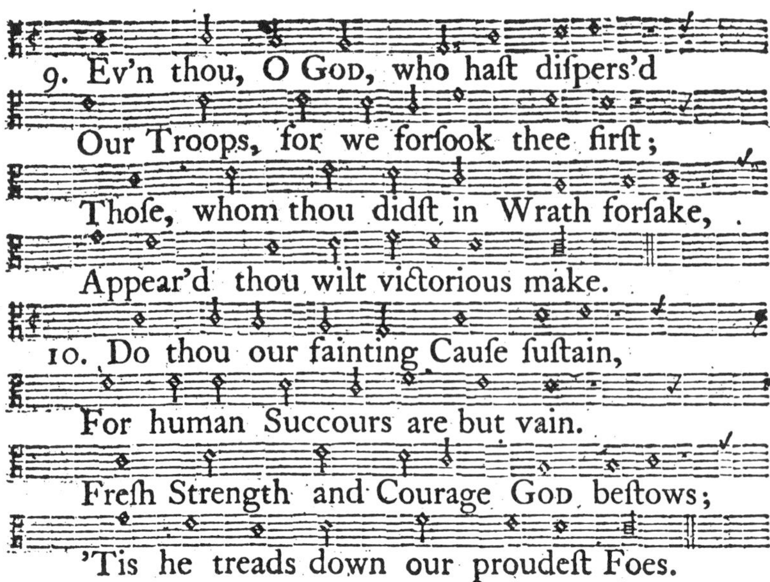
9. Ev'n thou, O God, who haſt diſpers'd
Our Troops, for we forſook thee firſt;
Thoſe, whom thou didſt in Wrath forſake,
Appear'd thou wilt victorious make.
10. Do thou our fainting Cauſe ſuſtain,
For human Succours are but vain.
Freſh Strength and Courage God beſtows;
'Tis he treads down our proudeſt Foes.

2. Choral Music in New England: Eighteenth and Early Nineteenth Centuries

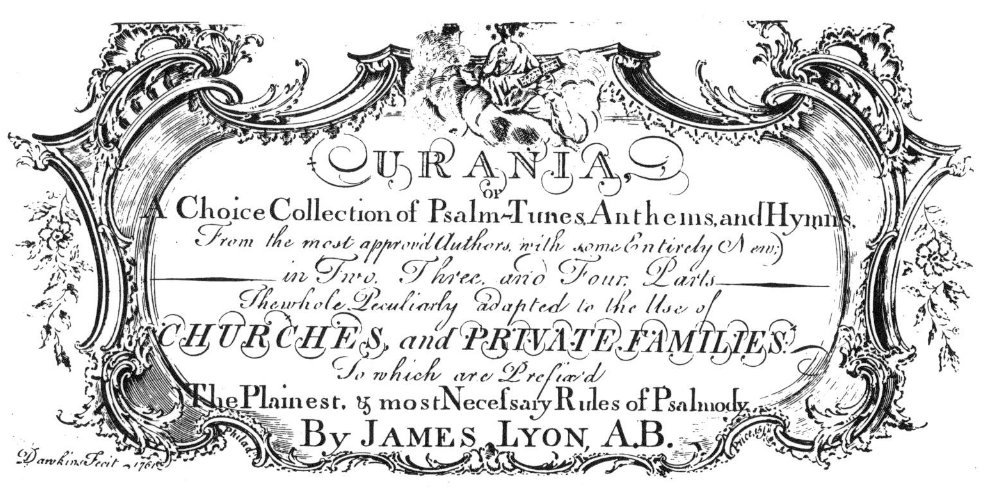

URANIA,
or
A Choice Collection of Psalm-Tunes, Anthems, and Hymns,
From the most approv'd Authors, with some Entirely New;
in Two, Three, and Four, Parts
The whole Peculiarly adapted to the Use of
CHURCHES, and PRIVATE FAMILIES.
To which are Prefix'd
The Plainest, & most Necessary Rules of Psalmody.
By JAMES LYON, A.B.

Philad.
Price 15/
Dawkins Fecit 1761

The 23.d Psalm Tune
Treble
Counter
Tenor
Bass

Two Celebrated Verses by Stemhold & Hopkins set to Music
Treble
The Lor......d descended from above. and bo.....w'd the heavens most high. bo.....w'd the
Bass
heavens most high: and underneath his feet, he cast the darkness, the darkness of the sky
The Lord descended from above and bow'd the heavens most high bow'd the heavens most high and
The Lord descended from above and bow'd the heavens most high bow'd the heavens most high and
underneath his feet he cast the darkness, the darkness of the sky.
Allegro
On cherubs & on cherubims full royal.
underneath his feet he cast the darkness, the darkness of the sky.
On cherubs & on cherubims full royal.

......ly herode, full roy-ally he rode.
oncherubs and oncherubims, full royal...ly herode.
......ly herode.
full royally herode.
he ro.......................................de. on cherubs and on cherubims, full
full royally herode, he ro.......................................de. on che...rubs and on che...rubims, full
roy.....ally he rode and on the wings of mighty winds came fly.........................ing all abroad
roy.....ally he rode and on the wings of mighty winds came fly.........................ing all abroad

on the wings.
on cherubs and on cherubims. full
on the wings.
on cherubs and on cherubims. full
on the wings of migh...... ty winds. on &c.
roy... ally he rode, and on the wings of mighty winds, came fly.... ing all abroad.
roy.... ally he rode, and on the wings of mighty winds, came fly...... ing all abroad.

AN ANTHEM FROM THE 114th PSALM.

Francis Hopkinson, 1760.

AN ANTHEM FROM THE 114th PSALM.

THE

The Singing Maſter's Aſſiſtant.

OR

Key to Practical Muſic.

BEING

An Abridgement from the New-England Pſalm-Singer; together with ſeveral other Tunes never before publiſhed.

Compoſed by WILLIAM BILLINGS,

AUTHOR OF THE NEW-ENGLAND PSALM-SINGER.

---

1 Chron. 15. 22. And Chenaniah chief of the Levites was for ſong: He inſtructed about the Song, becauſe he was ſkilful.
Ezra 7. 24. It ſhall not be lawful to impoſe Toll, Tribute, or Cuſtom upon Singers.
Nehemiah 11. 23. A certain Portion ſhould be for the Singers, due for every Day.
Prov. 17. 22. A merry Heart doeth good like a Medicine.

Majeſtic God our Muſe inſpire, and fill us with Seraphic Fire;
Augment, our Swells our Tones refine, Performance our's, the Glory Thine.

BOSTON: (NEW-ENGLAND.) PRINTED BY DRAPER AND FOLSOM 1778.

BOSTON. C.M.
Methinks I see a Heav'nly host, Of Angels on the wing, Methinks I hear their chearful notes So merrily they sing
Let all your fears be banish'd hence, Glad tidings we proclaim, For there's a Saviour born to day, And Jesus is his name
CHESTER. L.M.
Let tyrants shake their iron rod,
And Slav'ry clank her galling chains.
We fear them not we trust in God,
New-englands God forever reigns.
2
Howe and Burgoyne and Clinton too,
With Prescot and Cornwallis join'd,
Together plot our Overthrow,
In one Infernal league combin'd.
3
When God inspir'd us for the fight,
Their ranks were broke, their lines were forc'd,
Their Ships were Shatter'd in our sight
Or swiftly driven from our Coast.
The Foe comes on with haughty Stride
Our troops advance with martial noise,
Their Vet'runs flee before our Youth
And Gen'rals yield to beardless Boys.
5
What grateful Off'ring shall we bring
What shall we render to the Lord
Loud Hallelujahs let us Sing
JARGON.
Forte
Fortissimo
Let horrid Jargon split the Air And rive the Nerves asunder Let hateful Discord greet the Ear As ter ri ble as Thunder.

THE MISSOURI HARMONY,

OR A CHOICE COLLECTION OF

PSALM TUNES, HYMNS, AND ANTHEMS,

SELECTED FROM THE MOST EMINENT AUTHORS AND WELL ADAPTED TO ALL CHRISTIAN CHURCHES,

SINGING SCHOOLS, AND PRIVATE SOCIETIES.

TOGETHER WITH AN

INTRODUCTION TO GROUNDS OF MUSIC, THE RUDIMENTS OF MUSIC,

AND PLAIN RULES FOR BEGINNERS.

BY ALLEN D. CARDEN.

REVISED AND IMPROVED

CINCINNATI:

PRINTED AND PUBLISHED BY MORGAN AND SANXAY.

Stereotyped by Oliver Wells & Co.

1833.

THE ROSE OF SHARON.
I am the rose of Sharon, and the lilly of the vallies
I am the rose of Sharon, and the lilly of the vallies.
As the lily among the thorns, so is my love among the daughters.
As the apple tree the apple tree a- mong the trees of the wood.
so is my beloved among the sons, so is my beloved among the sons,
I sat down under his shadow with great delight.
And his fruit was sweet to my taste.
And his fruit, And his fruit was sweet to my taste.
And his fruit was sweet to my taste
And his fruit, and his fruit was sweet to my taste,
And his fruit, and his fruit, &c.
He brought me to the banqueting house
his banner over me was love.
He brought me to the banqueting house, his banner over me was love.
Stay me with flagons, comfort me with

apples, for I am sick, for I am sick, for I am sick of love, I charge you, O ye daughters of Jerusalem,
By the rose, and by the hinds of the field, that you stir not up, that you stir not up, that you stir not up, that you stir not up, nor a-
wake, awake awake awake my love till he please.
The voice of my beloved, Behold! he cometh,
leaping upon the mountains, skipping. leaping upon the mountains, skipping upon the hills.
My beloved spake, and
6
8
9
8
2
4

said unto me, rise up, rise up, rise up, riso up my love, my fair one and come a- way. For lo the winter is
past, the rain is over and gone. For lo, &c. the rain is over, the
rain is over, the rain is over and gone. For lo, &c.

JUDGMENT ANTHEM.

JUDGMENT ANTHEM, Continued.

JUDGMENT ANTHEM Continued.
in the air, Hallelujah, hallelujah, welcome, welcome bleeding Lamb. Now his merit by the harpers, Thro' the eternal deep resounds. Now re-
splendent shine his nail prints, ev'ry eye shall see the wound, They who pierced him shall at his appearance wail.
Ev'ry island, sea and mountain, Heav'n and earth shall flee away; All who hate him must ashamed Hear the trump proclaim the day, Come to judgment,
Come to judgment, Stand before the son of man: Hark, hark, the archangel swells the soleman summons loud,
Tears the strong pil-
Hark the shrill out-

lars of the vaults of heaven, Breaks up old marble, the repose of princes: See the graves open and the bones arising, Flames all around them.
cries of the guilty wretches, Lively bright horror and amazing anguish Stare thro' their eyelids: while the living worm, Lies gnawing within them.
Brisk.
Very Loud.
See the Judge's hand arising, Fill'd with vengeance on his foes.
Down to hell there's no redemption, Ev'ry Christless soul must go, Down to hell, depart, ye cursed into everlasting flames.
Very slow and Soft.
Brisk.
Lively and loud.
Hear the Saviour's words of mercy, Come ye ransom'd sinners home: Swift and joyful on your journey,
To the palace of your God.
See the souls that earth despised, In ce-
Joy celestial, hymns harmonious In soft
lestial glories move, Hallelujah big with wonder, Praising Christ's eternal love. Hallelujah, hallelujah echo through the realms of light.
symphony resound; Angels, seraphs, harps and trumpets, Swell the sweet angelic sound; Hail Almighty, Great eternal Lord, Amen.

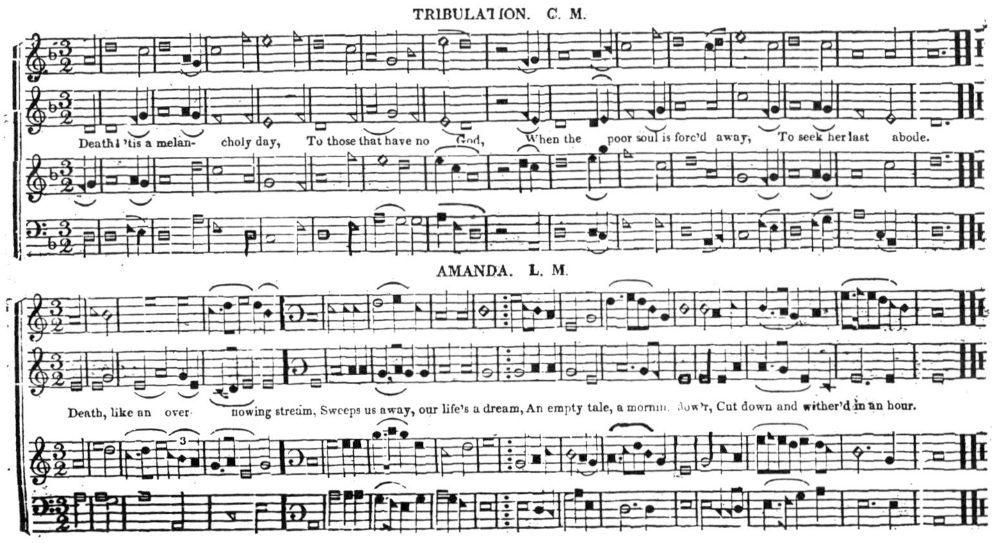
TRIBULATION. C. M.
Death! 'tis a melan- choly day, To those that have no God, When the poor soul is forc'd away, To seek her last abode.
AMANDA. L. M.
Death, like an over- flowing stream, Sweeps us away, our life's a dream, An empty tale, a mornin ow'r, Cut down and wither'd in an hour.

THE CHOIR:

OR

UNION COLLECTION OF CHURCH MUSIC.

CONSISTING OF A GREAT VARIETY OF

PSALM AND HYMN TUNES, ANTHEMS, &c.

Original and Selected.

INCLUDING MANY BEAUTIFUL SUBJECTS FROM THE WORKS OF

Haydn, Mozart, Cherubini, Nauman, Marcello, Mehul, Himmel, Winter, Weber, Rossini, and other eminent composers,

HARMONIZED AND ARRANGED EXPRESSLY FOR THIS WORK.

BY LOWELL MASON,

Professor in the Boston Academy of Music ; Editor of Handel and Haydn Society Collection of Church Music, Choral Harmony, Lyra Sacra, &c.

SECOND EDITION.

Boston:

CARTER, HENDEE AND CO.

131 Washington street.

1833.

Price, $10 per dozen.

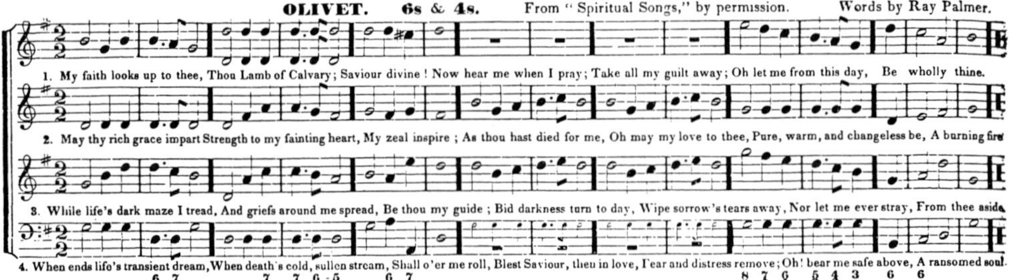
OLIVET. 6s & 4s. From "Spiritual Songs," by permission. Words by Ray Palmer.
1. My faith looks up to thee, Thou Lamb of Calvary; Saviour divine! Now hear me when I pray; Take all my guilt away; Oh let me from this day, Be wholly thine.
2. May thy rich grace impart Strength to my fainting heart, My zeal inspire; As thou hast died for me, Oh may my love to thee, Pure, warm, and changeless be, A burning fire!
3. While life's dark maze I tread, And griefs around me spread, Be thou my guide; Bid darkness turn to day, Wipe sorrow's tears away, Nor let me ever stray, From thee aside.
4. When ends life's transient dream, When death's cold, sullen stream, Shall o'er me roll, Blest Saviour, then in love, Fear and distress remove; Oh! bear me safe above, A ransomed soul.

Published under the Sanction of the Boston Academy of Music.

CARMINA SACRA:

OR

BOSTON COLLECTION OF CHURCH MUSIC.

COMPRISING THE MOST POPULAR

PSALM AND HYMN TUNES IN GENERAL USE,

TOGETHER WITH A GREAT VARIETY OF

NEW TUNES, CHANTS, SENTENCES, MOTETTS, AND ANTHEMS,

PRINCIPALLY BY DISTINGUISHED EUROPEAN COMPOSERS:

THE WHOLE CONSTITUTING

ONE OF THE MOST COMPLETE COLLECTIONS OF MUSIC

FOR CHOIRS, CONGREGATIONS, SINGING SCHOOLS AND SOCIETIES, EXTANT.

SECOND EDITION.

BY LOWELL MASON,

PROFESSOR IN THE BOSTON ACADEMY OF MUSIC; EDITOR OF THE BOSTON HANDEL AND HAYDN COLLECTION OF CHURCH MUSIC, THE CHOIR OR UNION COLLECTION, THE BOSTON ACADEMY'S COLLECTION, THE MODERN PSALMIST, AND VARIOUS OTHER MUSICAL WORKS.

BOSTON:

PUBLISHED BY J. H. WILKINS & R. B. CARTER.

NEW YORK:—F. J. HUNTINGTON & CO., ROBINSON, PRATT & CO., AND COLLINS, KEESE & CO.

PHILADELPHIA:—THOMAS, COWPERTHWAIT & CO., AND HENRY PERKINS.

1841.

MISSIONARY HYMN. 7s & 6s.

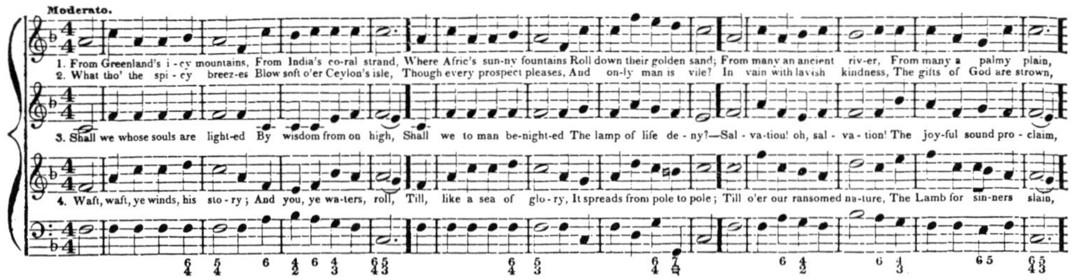

MUSICA SACRA:

OR

SPRINGFIELD AND UTICA COLLECTIONS

UNITED:

CONSISTING OF

PSALM AND HYMN TUNES, ANTHEMS AND CHANTS;

ARRANGED FOR TWO, THREE OR FOUR VOICES, WITH A FIGURED BASS FOR THE ORGAN OR PIANO FORTE.

BY THOMAS HASTINGS AND SOLOMON WARRINER.

REVISED EDITION

UTICA:

PRINTED AND PUBLISHED BY WILLIAM WILLIAMS,

No. 60, Genesee Street.

1818.

ORDINATION ANTHEM. *T. Hastings.*

Alto.
As for our Re - deem - er, As for, &c. the Lord of Hosts
Pia. For.
As for our Redeemer. Sym. the Lord, &c.
is his name the Ho - - ly One of Isra - - - el.
the Ho - ly One, &c.
Alto.
he hath borne our griefs,
2d Treble.
Pia. Mod. Affet. Expressivo.
Surely, He hath borne our griefs, and carried our

He died for us. Being ris'n
Cres.
sorrows, He died for us. Being ris'n
from the dead, He di - eth no more.
from the dead, He di - eth no more.
2d Treble.
O ye gates, lift up your heads, O ye
Spirituoso.
O ye gates, &c.
Sym.

gates, lift up your heads, And be ye lifted up, ye ev - erlast - ing
ye ev - erlast - ing
unisons.
doors, And let the King of Glo - ry en - - ter.
Single Voice.
Who
doors, the King, &c.
Sym.
is he? Who is he? The King of Glo - ry, the Lord,
strong, and mighty, the Lord, mighty in Battle.

2d Treble.
O ye gates, lift up your heads, O ye gates, &c.
Single Voice.
And be ye lifted up, ye everlasting doors. Who
Sym.
Unisons.
is he? Who is he? the King of Glory.
CHORUS. Tenor.
Je - ho - vah of Hosts, Je - ho - - vah of Hosts. He,
2d Treble.
Pomposo.
Je - ho - vah of Hosts, Je - ho - vah of Hosts, He,

He is the King, He is the King of Glo - ry, the King of Glo - - ry.
He is the King, He is the King of Glo - ry, the King of Glo - - ry.
How beautiful are the feet,
How beautiful, How beautiful, are the feet of
Grazioso.
Sym.
How, &c. How, &c.
him that publisheth that publisheth salvation, How beautiful how.
How, &c. of him &c.
8v.

Cry a - loud, spare not, lift up thy voice like a trumpet
Cry a loud, spare not, lift up thy voice. Show my people
beautiful, cry a loud, cry a loud,
publisheth, cry a loud, cry a loud, show my people
their transgressions, Show, &c.
their transgressions, Show, &c.
Woe, woe to the wicked. Say un - to the
Vivace.
Woe, woe to the wicked. Say un - to the

Righteous, it shall be well with him. it shall, &c.
Righteous, it shall be well with him. it shall, &c.
6
5
6
5
6
5

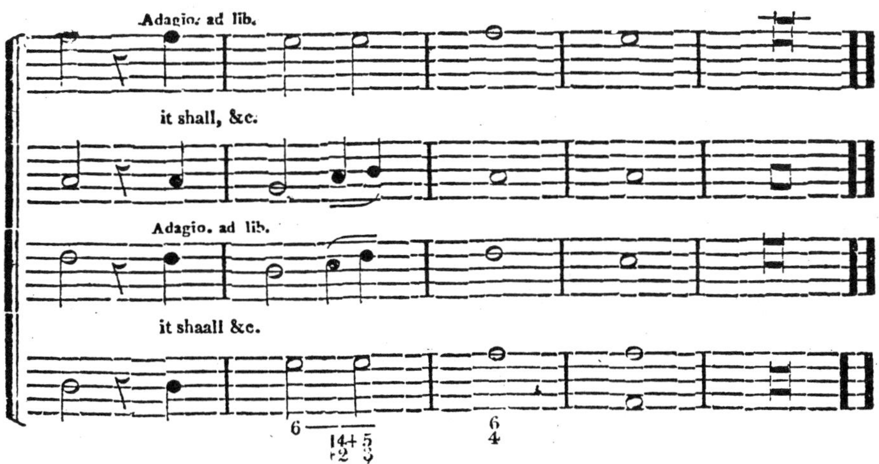
Adagio, ad lib.
it shall, &c.
Adagio. ad lib.
it shaall &c.
6
6
4

DEDICATION. T. Hastings.
[An occasional piece composed in a familiar style.]
Tenor.
A - rise, O King of grace, a - - rise, And enter to thy
2d Treble.
Air. Soave.
A - rise, O King of grace, a - - rise, And enter to thy
unisons.
rest, A - rise, A - - rise, And enter to thy
Pia. For. Pia.
rest, A - - rise, O King of grace, a - - rise, And enter to thy
rest, Thus to be own'd and
Lo thy church waits with longing eyes, Thus to be own'd and
rest,

1st time.
Fine.
bless'd. Thus to be own'd and bless'd. Thus, &c.
1st time.
Fine.
bless'd.
For. 1st time.
Fine.
Thus to be own'd and bless'd. Thus, &c.
1st time.
Fine.
Enter with all thy glorious train, En - ter with all thy glorious train, Thy Spirit and thy
All that the ark did once contain, All that the ark did once contain, Could no such grace af-
Enter with all thy glorious train, Enter with all thy glorious train, Thy Spirit and thy
All that the ark did once contain, All that the ark did once contain, Could no such grace af-
word.
ford.
All that the ark did once contain, Could no such grace afford. Could, &c.
word.
ford.
All that the ark did once contain, Could no such grace afford. Could no, &c.
2d time.
1st time.

Here repeat the second strain in the fourth verse, and then close with the first strain.

4 Here let the son of David reign,
Let God's anointed shine;
Justice and truth his court maintain,
With love and pow'r divine.

3. Shape-Note and Gospel Hymns in the Midwest and South

THE EASY INSTRUCTOR;

OR,

A NEW METHOD OF TEACHING

Sacred Harmony.

CONTAINING,

I. THE RUDIMENTS OF MUSIC on an improved Plan, wherein the Naming and Timing of the Notes are familiarized to the weakest Capacity.

II. A choice Collection of PSALM TUNES and ANTHEMS, from the most celebrated Authors, with a number composed in Europe and America, entirely new; suited to all the Metres sung in the different Churches in the United States.

Published for the Use of SINGING SOCIETIES in general, but more particularly for those who have not the advantage of an INSTRUCTOR.

BY WILLIAM LITTLE AND WILLIAM SMITH.

PRINTED, TYPOGRAPHICALLY, AT ALBANY,

BY WEBSTERS & SKINNER AND DANIEL STEELE, (Proprietors of the Copy-Right,)

And sold at their respective Book Stores, at the corner of State and Pearl-Streets, and a few doors south of the Old City-Hall, in Court-Street; by T. & J. SWORDS, EVERET DUYCKINCK and WILLIAM FALCONER, *New-York*; WM. J. M'CARTEE, *Schenectady*; A. SEWARD, *Utica*; TRACY & BLISS, *Lansingburgh*; PARKER & BLISS, *Troy*; INCREASE COOK, *New-Haven*; M. CARY, *Philadelphia*; J. BOGERT, *Geneva*; J. D. BEMIS, *Canandaigua*; P. POTTER, *Poughkeepsie*; E. LEWIS, *Newburgh*, and D. ALLENSON & Co. *Burlington, N. J.*

O. R. VAN BENTHUYSEN, TYPOGRAPHER.

INDEX.

ADVERTISEMENT.

AS the Authors are well aware, that whatever has the appearance of novelty is, from this very circumstance, in danger of meeting with an unfavorable reception; they request nothing more than a critical observation of the certificate annexed, and an impartial examination of the method proposed, being willing to submit it to the merit of the performance to the determination of the candid and judicious. As the introduction of the four singing syllables, by characters, shewing at sight, the name of the notes, may perhaps be considered as subjecting those who are taught in this manner to difficulty in understanding other books, without this assistance—the authors would just observe, that if pupils are made acquainted with the principle here laid down, the objection will be found, by experience, more specious than solid. To this it might be added, that in the old way, there are not less than seven different ways of applying the four singing syllables to the lines and spaces, which is attended with great difficulty: But this difficulty is entirely removed upon the present plan; and we know of know objection to this plan, unless that it is not in use; which objection is no objection at all, or at least, cannot be decisive, as this would give currency to the entire rejection and exclusion of all improvements whatever. And as the novelty of a singing book rendered so easy, from its improvements, that any person of a tolerable voice might actually learn the art of psalmody without an instructor, if they could but obtain the sounds of the eight notes, which has lead its advocates to request a publication of the same. We have, therefore, the pleasure to inform the public, that since, subscriptions have been in circulation for this book, we have been honored with upwards of three thousand subscribers; In consequence of which we flatter ourselves, that this book will meet with a kind reception.

Philadelphia, August 15th, 1798. George W. Tucker. Tuckerton N.J.

WILLIAM LITTLE,
WILLIAM SMITH.

The Committee appointed by the URANIAN SOCIETY of Philadelphia, to examine a SINGING BOOK, entitled,

"THE EASY INSTRUCTOR," BY WILLIAM LITTLE,

REPORT....That having carefully examined the same, they find it contains a well digested system of principles and rules, and a judicous collection of tunes: And from the improvement of having only four significant characters, indicating, at sight, the names of the notes, and a sliding rule for timing the same, this book is considered easier to be learned than any we have seen.

Were it possible to acquire the sound of the eight notes but by imitation, they verily believe they might be obtained by the help of this book even without an instructor.

The committe are of opinion, the Author merits the patronage and encouragement of all friends to Church Music:

EDWARD STAMMERS,
RICHARD T. LEECH.

George W. Tucker. Tuckerton
New Jersey.

PREFACE.

THE song of praise is an act of devotion so becoming, delightful and excellent, that we find it coeval with the sense of Deity authorized by the example of all nations, and universally received into the solemnities of public worship. Under the *Jewish Dispensation*, the Holy Spirit of God directed this expression of homage, as peculiarly becoming the *place where his honor dwelleth*. The book of *Psalms*, as the name itself imports, was adapted to the voice of song ; and the author of those invaluable odes well knew the sweetness, dignity, and animation that were hereby added to the sacred service of the temple. With what rapture do they describe its effects—with what fervor do they call upon their fellow worshippers to join in this delightful duty.—*It is a good thing to give thanks unto the Lord, and to sing praises unto thy name, O thou Most High. Praise ye the Lord for it is good to sing praises unto our God ; for it is pleasant, and praise is comely. O sing unto the Lord a new song—sing unto the Lord all the earth—sing unto the Lord—bless his name—shew forth his salvation from day to day.* Nor hath Christianity dispensed with religious song as an unmeaning ceremony, or an unprofitable sacrifice. It commands us to address the Father *in spirit and in truth* ; but it nevertheless enjoins those outward acknowledgments that fitly express and cherish the pious temper. Our blessed Lord was pleased to consecrate this act of worship by his own example, under circumstances the most effecting. He concluded the celebration of that supper, which was the memorial of his dying love, by an hymn of praise. And his apostles frequently exhorted to the observation of this duty ;—*Let the word of God dwell in you richly in all wisdom ; teaching and admonishing one another in psalms, and hymns, and spiritual songs ; singing with grace in your hearts unto the Lord.*

DIVINE song is undoubtedly the language of nature : It originates from our frame and constitution : Do lofty contemplations, elevated joy and fervor of affection, give beauty and dignity to language, and associate with the charms of poetry, by a kindred law which the Creator hath established—They pleasingly unite with strains of sweet and solemn harmony. And there are two principal views, in which music will appear to render eminent service to the sacrifice of praise :—In the first place, it suitably expresses the sentiments of devotion, and the sublime delight which religion is fitted to inspire. Joy is the natural effect of praise, and song the proper accompaniment of joy. *Is any merry* or glad *let him sing psalms* ; and singing is not only a general indication of delight, but expressive, also, of the prevailing sentiments and passions of the mind—it can accommodate itself to the various modifications of love and joy, the essence of a devotional temper—it hath lofty strains for the sublimity of admiration—plaintive accents, which become the tear of penitence and sorrow—it can adopt the humble plea of supplication, or swell the bolder notes of thanksgiving and triumph : Yet it hath been properly remarked, that the influence of song reaches only to the amiable and pleasing affections, and that it hath no expression for malignant and tormenting passions ; the sorrow, therefore, to which it is attuned, should be mingled with hope—the penitence which it expresses, cheered with the sense of pardon, and the mournful scenes on which it sometimes dwells, irradiated with the glorious views and consolations of the gospel.

In the second place, music not only decently expresses, but powerfully EXCITES and IMPROVES the devout affections ; it is the prerogative of this noble art to cheer and invigorate the mind—to still the tumultuous passions—to calm the troubled thoughts, and to fix the wandering attention : And hereby it happily composes and prepares the heart for the exercise of public worship. But it further boasts a wondrous efficacy in leading to that peculiar temper which becomes the subject of praise, and is favorable to religious impression. It can strike the mind with solemnity and awe, or melt with tenderness and love—can animate with hope and gladness, or call forth the sensations of devout and affectionate sorrows ; even separate and unconnected, it can influence the various passions and movements of the soul ; but it naturally seeks an alliance, and must be joined with becoming sentiments and language, in order to produce its full and proper effect ; and never is its energy so conspicuous and delightful, as when consecrated to the service of religion, and employed in the courts of the living God—Here it displays its noblest use, and its brightest glory ; here alone it meets with theams that fill the capacity of an immortal mind, and claims its noblest powers and affections. What voice of song so honorable, so elevating and delightful ? To whom shall the breath ascend in melodious accents, if not to him who first inspired it? Where shall admiration take her loftiest flight, but to the throne of the everlasting Jehovah ? Or what shall *awake our glory*, and kindle our warmest gratitude, if not the remembrance of his daily mercies, and the praise of redeeming love ? When the union of the heart and voice are thus happily arranged—when sublime subjects of praise are accompanied with expressive harmony, and the pleasure of genuine devotion heightened by the charms of singing, we participate of the most pure, rational, noble and exquisite enjoyments that human nature is capable of receiving :—The soul forgets the confinement with the body, is elevated beyond the cares and tumults of this mortal state, and seems for a while transported to the blissful regions of perfect love and joy : And it is worthy of remark, that the sacred writings delight to represent the heavenly felicity under this image : And though such language be allowed to be figurative—though *eye hath not seen, nor ear heard, neither hath it entered into the heart of man to conceive the things God hath prepared for them that love him* ; yet our most natural—our most just conceptions of the happiness of the heavenly world, is that which we have been describing, viz. sublime devotion accompanied with rapturous delight.

The human mind is not only capable of extensive knowledge, but is incapable of being entirely in a state of supineness : This thirst for happiness implanted in the human breast, must have some object for its pursuit ; therefore the Almighty has made us capable of enjoying pure and intellectual pleasures ; and we find if improvements are neglected among young people, their manners at once, verge towards heathenism. And since it is impracticable, for any, entirely to separate their children from meeting among young people, those who wish to promote civilization, will see the importance of bending the young mind to something that will ornament and refine society, even if they have a separate design in it. The funds of knowledge in the minds of most young people, are not sufficient to carry on a discourse to any considerable length ; therefore, we find that their evenings are often spent in a very simple manner, nothing more will be heard than insignificant jokes, and vulgarism seems to be the highest entertainment ; but when they have tasted the more pure pleasures, such as flow from music, the young circle seems to look with contempt on the former manner in which they spent their time, which then seemed to hover them over the summit of bliss. But besides the more immediate propriety and use of divine song in the ordinances of religion, its indirect advantages have a claim to our regard. It is not only in itself delightful and profitable, but it gives animation to other parts of public worship—it revives the attention—recruits the exhausted spirits, and begets a happy composure and tranquility. It is peculiarly agreeable as a social act, and that in which every person may be imployed. Nor is it the least of its benefits, that it associates pleasing ideas with divine worship, and makes us *glad when we go into the house of the Lord.* It is also a bond of union in religious societies, promotes the regular attendance of their members, and seldom fails of adding to their numbers : But there seems to be something more in music to unite with our own experience and the wisdom of past ages. The early Christians found their account in a remarkable attachment to psalmody, and almost every rising sect have availed themselves of its important delights and advantages. It must be confessed that where pleasure is the sole attention the motive is of an inferior nature. But is it not a commendable policy to promote regular attendance upon places of worship, by any means that are not reprehensible ? Will not the most beneficial consequences probably ensue ? Is there not every reason to expect that persons who frequent the house of God with this view alone, will not be uninterested in the other services of religion ?—That they who come to sing may learn to pray—that they whose only wish it was to be entertained, may find themselves instructed and improved? Such is the happy tendency of well regulated song in the house of God ; but alas ! how seldom is this part of the service accompanied with its proper effect.. It was the remark of an eminent writer, too applicable to the present time, that "The worship in which we should most resemble the inhabitants of heaven, is the worst performed upon earth." His pious labors have greatly enriched the matter of song, and hereby contributed to remove one cause of this complaint ; but in the manner there still remains a miserable defect.—Too often does a disgraceful silence prevail to the utter neglect of this duty—too often are dissonance and discord substituted for the charms of melody and harmony, and the singing performed in a way so carelessly and indecently, that as the same writer observes, "instead of elevating our devotions to the most divine and delightful sensations, it awakens our regret, and touches all the strings of uneasiness within us." But is this owing to causes which cannot be removed, or doth it not imply reproach and blame ? Will not truth oblige us to confess, that the fault rests not in a want of natural taste and abilities, nor of sufficient leisure, but in a great carelessness and neglect ? Moderate attention and application would surmount every difficulty, and lead to a suitable proficiency in this happy art. An exercise so pleasing and attractive, seems only to want regulation and method.

Time.

THE two first modes in Common Time have four beats in a bar, and may be performed in the following manner, viz. The first beat strike the end of the fingers on what you beat upon ; the second beat, bring down the heel of the hand ; the third beat, raise the hand half way up ; the fourth beat, raise the hand clear up. The third and fourth modes of Common, and the first and second of Compound Time, have but two beats in a bar, and the best method we know of measuring time in these four modes, is by beating with the hand, saying one with it down, and two with up.

To arrive at an exactness in this mode of calculating, the learner may beat by the motion of a pendulum vibrating in a second, without paying any regard to the notes. For by this method he will become habituated to regularity and exact proportion.

BEATING of time should be attended to before any attempt to sounding the notes is made. Counting and beating frequently while learning the rules, will be of great service. A large motion of the hand is best at first, but as soon as the learner can beat with accuracy, a small motion is sufficient.

To attain to exactness, it will be necessary that the learner should name and beat the time of notes in each bar, both of the eight notes and a number of the plain tunes in the different modes of time set to the eight notes in this performance, without sounding, until a perfect knowledge of their variety is obtained ; After which, he may proceed to those that are more complex and difficult.

HAVING complied with these directions, the learner will acquire the time of the notes with much greater ease and exactness, than if his attention was directed to three things at once--the name, the time and the sound of the notes.

As much depends on a proper knowledge of time, I would recommend to teachers to make use of a sliding rule, or something that will cover the notes, so as to admit to the view of the pupil only such note or notes, as shall determine the first half of a bar at a time ; by which means they will acquire exactness in beating, and give to each its due proportion.

This may be considered by some as a useless novelty, but we can assure them, from long experience, that the effect will convince them of its being worthy of attention, and much the quickest and easiest method to ascertain the exact time of the notes.

Of Managing the Voice.

IF directions, given by ancient and modern critics (for the modulating of the voice) to those who are desirous of excelling in public speaking are necessary, directions are particularly requisite to enable the student in music, to sing with grace and energy ; therefore,

1st. ABOVE all things affectation should be guarded against—for whilst it is contrary to that humility which ever ought to characterise the devout worshiper, it must be an enemy to the natural ease which always distinguishes the judicious performance.

2d. CARE should be taken to begin with a proper pitch of the voice, otherwise it is impossible to preserve the melodious connexion of the notes, or the harmony of the parts ; for if at the commencement of a tune the voice is too low, langor must prevail ; if too high, an unnatural endeavor to maintain a proportioned elevation throughout the whole performance.

3d. THE articulation must be as distinct as the sound will possibly admit ; for in this, vocal music has the preference of instrumental—that while the ear is delighted, the mind is informed.

4th. THOUGH it is the opinion of most writers, that the learners should take the parts best adapted to their respective voices ; let them occasionally try the differnt parts ; not only because it makes them better acquainted with the nature and degrees of sounds, but because it has a tendency to improve the voice, to file off what is too rough, and what is too effeminate to render more energetic ; whereas monotony, is otherwise, apt to take place. By attending to this direction the evil will be greatly guarded against.

5th. THOSE who have but indifferent voices, will find great benefit, if after faithfully trying an easy tune themselves, they can get a good singer to sing with them ; and by attending to his performance they will instantly perceive a difference--the ear will soon experience a pleasing superiority, and the learner, at every succeeding effort, will find that his mechanical sensibility, if we may be allowed the expression, is greatly improved.

General Observations.

THE learner must endeavor to know the characters, with their time in the eight notes. Learning twenty or thirty of the plain tunes well by note, before he attempts to sing by word, after which he may sing them over by word.

IN keeping time on the rests, or silent beats, I would recommend not to count the whole, and thus commit them to memory ; but to beat one bar at a time, and thus continue throughout the tune. This we find, is the most easy and accurate method of keeping time on the rests, particularly fuged tunes.

TEACHERS commit an imperceptible error in singing too much with their pupils, and in allowing them to unite in concert, before they can readily name and time the notes themselves, without assistance. If voices are ever so good there can be no music, were ignorance in these particular occasions frequent interruption. This mortifying circumstance has induced us to try this experiment of gaining fluency in naming the notes, and an accuracy in keeping of time, before we sufferd our pupils to attempt to unite in the parts ; and the effect convinced us that it is the most effectual method to correct the error ; which we flatter ourselves all who make trial of, will find it to exceed their most sanguine expectations.

THE high notes in all parts should be sung soft and clear, but not faint ; The low notes full and bold, but not harsh. The best general rule of singing in concert is, for each individual to sing so soft as to hear distinctly the other parts. The practice of singing soft will be greatly to the advantage of the learner, not only from the opportunity it will give him of hearing and imitating his teacher, but it is the best, and most ready way of cultivating his own, and making it melodious.

WHEN music is repeated, the sound should increase together with the emphasis : In tunes that repeat, the strength of voice should increase in the parts engaged, while the others are falling in with spirit ; in which case, the pronunciation should be as distinct and emphatical as possible.

WHEN singing in concert, no one, except the teacher or leader, should attempt a solo which does not belong to the part which he is singing ; it destroys the very intent of the composition, and intimates to the audience, that the person or persons, to whom the solo particularly belongs, was inadequate to the performance.

ALL solos should be sung softer than the parts when moving together.

NOTES tied with each other, should be sung softer than when one note answers to a syllable, and should be swelled in the throat, with the teeth and lips a little assunder, and sung if possible to one breath, which should be taken previously, at the beginning of each slur which is continued to any considerable length.

To obtain the true sounds of the intervals, the learner will find great advantage by repeating the sound over and over from the last notes he is attempting to sound, until he can obtain the sounds he would wish to retain : Proceeding in this manner, an indifferent voice may be greatly cultivated, when a hasty performance would not only be to no advantage, but discouraging indeed.

The Modes of Time expressed by Figures.

THE under figure shews into how may parts the semibreve is divided, and the upper figure shews how many of the same parts fill a bar. In the first mode of treble time, $\frac{3}{2}$, the upper figure shews that there are three notes contained in a bar ; the lower figure determines that they are minims, because two of them make a semibreve. Also, in the second mode, $\frac{3}{4}$, the upper figure shews you there are three notes contained in a bar ; the lower one that they are crotchets, because four of them will make one semibreve. And so all other modes, which are expressed by figures according to their marks.

PROPRIETY in accenting is rather to be acquired by example than precept ; therefore, teachers ought to be exceedingly attentive to this particular : For much of the beauty and energy of music depends upon proper emphasis. To accent such notes as fall on accented syllables, or emphatical words, let them fall on which part of the bar they may, is the best and most natural rule, and the highest perfection of accent. There are several other graces, which have a pleasing effect when executed in an accurate manner ; but as they are entirely impracticable for learners,

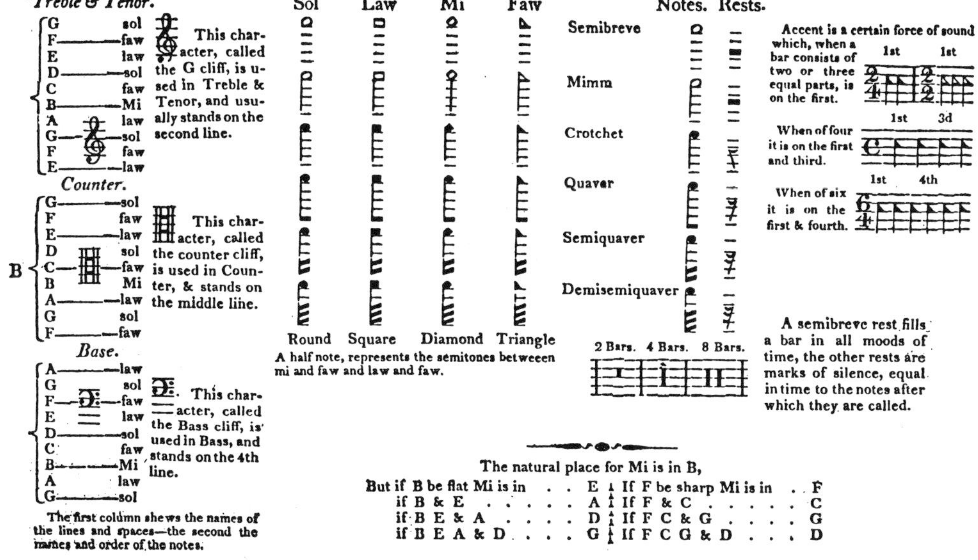

The natural place for Mi is in B,

But if B be flat Mi is in	E	If F be sharp Mi is in	F
if B & E	A	If F & C	C
if B E & A	D	If F C & G	G
if B E A & D	G	If F C G & D	D

A SCALE OF NOTES AND THEIR PROPORTION.

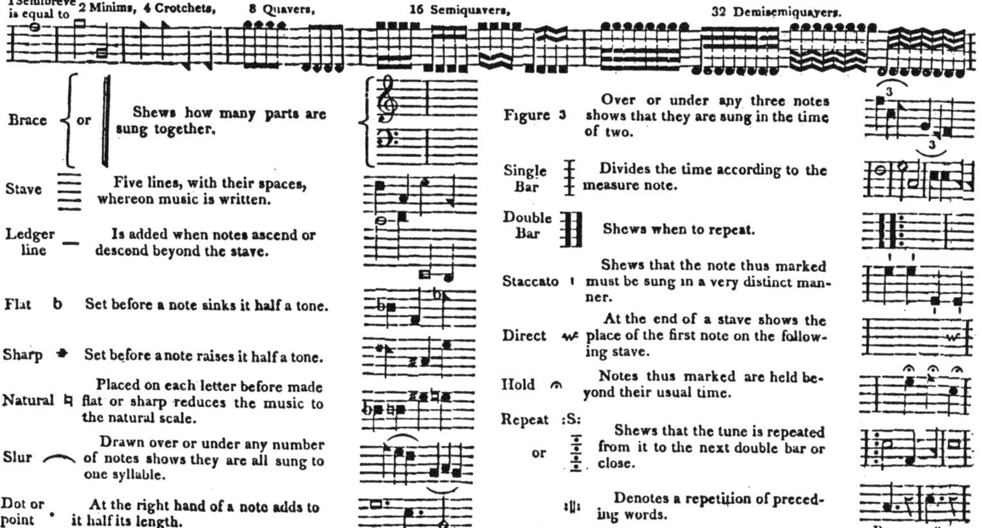

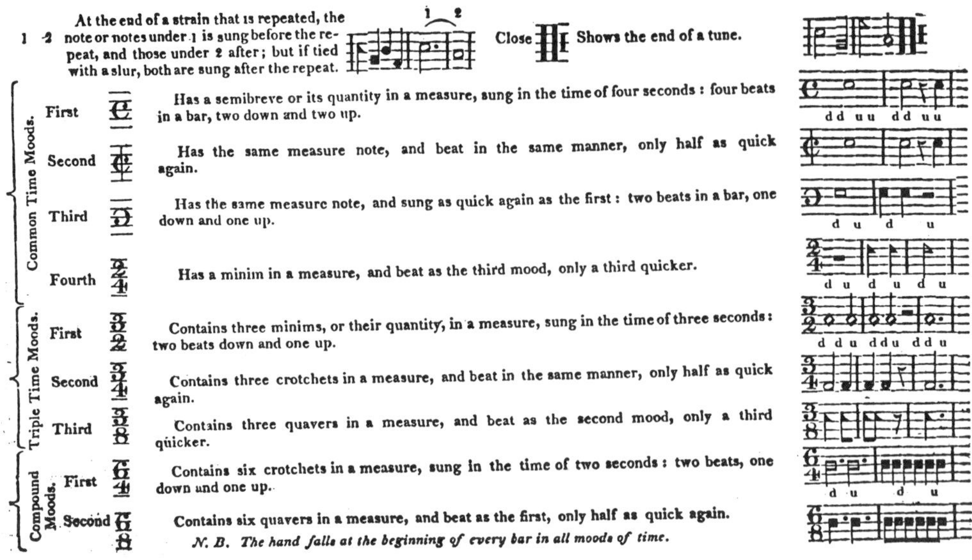
1 2 At the end of a strain that is repeated, the note or notes under 1 is sung before the repeat, and those under 2 after; but if tied with a slur, both are sung after the repeat.
1 2
Close Shows the end of a tune.
Common Time Moods.
First Has a semibreve or its quantity in a measure, sung in the time of four seconds: four beats in a bar, two down and two up.
d d u u d d u u
Second Has the same measure note, and beat in the same manner, only half as quick again.
Third Has the same measure note, and sung as quick again as the first: two beats in a bar, one down and one up.
d u d u
Fourth Has a minim in a measure, and beat as the third mood, only a third quicker.
d u d u d u
Triple Time Moods.
First Contains three minims, or their quantity, in a measure, sung in the time of three seconds: two beats down and one up.
d d u d d u d d u
Second Contains three crotchets in a measure, and beat in the same manner, only half as quick again.
Third Contains three quavers in a measure, and beat as the second mood, only a third quicker.
Compound Moods.
First Contains six crotchets in a measure, sung in the time of two seconds: two beats, one down and one up.
d u d u
Second Contains six quavers in a measure, and beat as the first, only half as quick again.
N. B. The hand falls at the beginning of every bar in all moods of time.

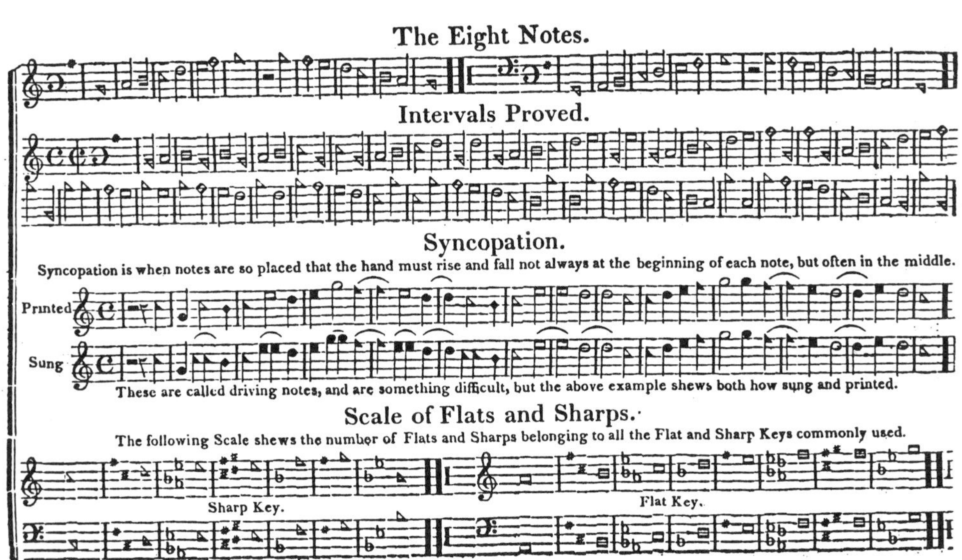
The Eight Notes.
Intervals Proved.
Syncopation.
Syncopation is when notes are so placed that the hand must rise and fall not always at the beginning of each note, but often in the middle.
Printed
Sung
These are called driving notes, and are something difficult, but the above example shews both how sung and printed.
Scale of Flats and Sharps.
The following Scale shews the number of Flats and Sharps belonging to all the Flat and Sharp Keys commonly used.
Sharp Key.
Flat Key.

BATH. L. M. Sharp Key on A.
Nature with open volume stands, To spread her Maker's praise abroad; And ev'ry labor of his hands, Shews something worthy of a God.
TWENTY-FIFTH. S. M. Flat Key on A.
I lift my soul to God, My trust is in his name ; Let not my foes that seek my blood, Still triumph in my shame.

THE

ART OF SINGING;

IN THREE PARTS:

TO WIT,

I. THE MUSICAL PRIMER,
II. THE CHISTIAN HARMONY,
III. THE MUSICAL MAGAZINE.

BY ANDREW LAW.

FOURTH EDITION WITH ADDITIONS AND IMPROVEMENTS.
PRINTED UPON A NEW PLAN.

PRINTED AT CAMBRIDGE, BY W. HILLIARD. 1893.

DELAWARE. No. 50.

Cheerful.

Let earth with every isle and sea Rejoice, the Saviour reigns; His word like fire prepares his way, And mountains melt to plains, And mountains,

OLD 100 No. 51.

Cheerful.

Ye nations round the earth, rejoice Before the Lord your sovereign King; Serve him with cheerful heart and voice, With all your tongues his glory sing.

THE MISSOURI HARMONY,

OR A CHOICE COLLECTION OF

PSALM TUNES, HYMNS, AND ANTHEMS,

SELECTED FROM THE MOST EMINENT AUTHORS AND WELL ADAPTED TO ALL CHRISTIAN CHURCHES,

SINGING SCHOOLS, AND PRIVATE SOCIETIES.

TOGETHER WITH AN

INTRODUCTION TO GROUNDS OF MUSIC, THE RUDIMENTS OF MUSIC,

AND PLAIN RULES FOR BEGINNERS.

BY ALLEN D. CARDEN.

REVISED AND IMPROVED.

CINCINNATI:

PRINTED AND PUBLISHED BY MORGAN AND SANXAY.

Stereotyped by Oliver Wells & Co.

1833.

CHINA. C. M.
Why do we mourn departing friends, Or shake at death's alarms? 'Tis but the voice that Jesus sends, To call them to his arms.

NORTHFIELD. C. M.
How long, dear Saviour, O how long shall this bright hour delay! Fly swifter round ye wheels of time, And bring the welcome day.

Gospel Hymns

Nos. 1 to 6 Complete

BY

Ira D. Sankey

James McGranahan and Geo. C. Stebbins

(DIAMOND EDITION)

The John Church Co.
CINCINNATI
CHICAGO | NEW YORK

The Biglow & Main Co.
135 FIFTH AVENUE, NEW YORK
LAKESIDE BUILDING, CHICAGO

A Soldier of the Cross.

"A good soldier of Jesus Christ."—2 Tim. 2: 3.

Isaac Watts. Ira D. Sankey.

Blessed Assurance.

"He that believeth on me hath everlasting life."—JOHN 6: 47.

FANNY J. CROSBY. MRS. JOSEPH F. KNAPP.

4. African-American Music

SLAVE SONGS

of the

UNITED STATES

BY

WILLIAM FRANCIS ALLEN

CHARLES PICKARD WARE

LUCY McKIM GARRISON

New York

PETER SMITH

1951

THE GOOD OLD WAY.

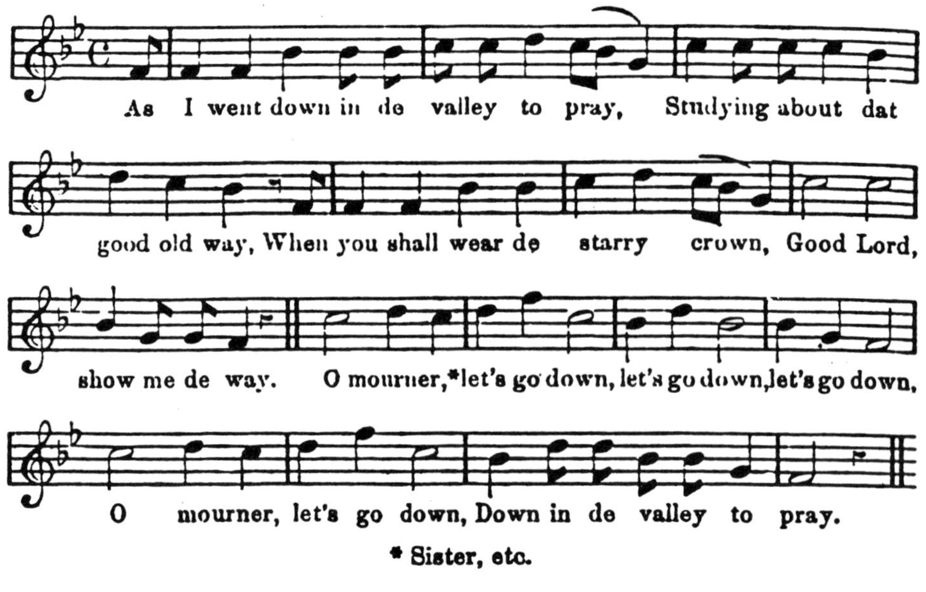

I'M GOING HOME.

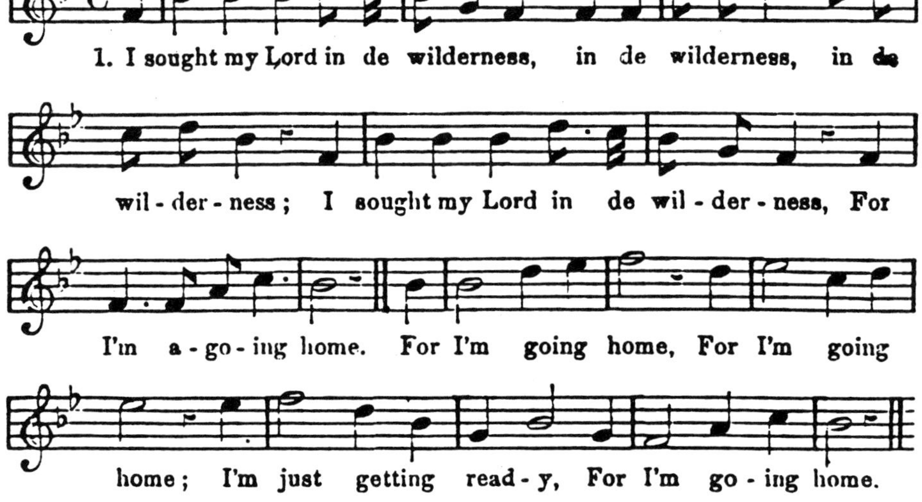

2 I found free grace in the wilderness,

3 My father preaches in the wilderness.

SINNER WON'T DIE NO MORE.

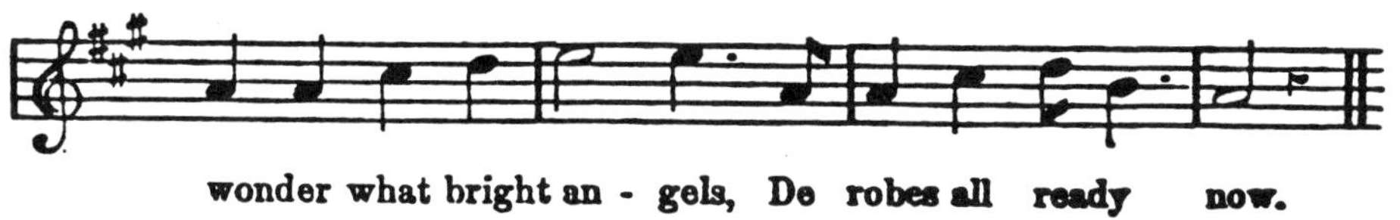

2 O see dem ships come a-sailing, sailing, sailing,
O see dem ships come a-sailing,
De robes all ready now.

THESE ARE ALL MY FATHER'S CHILDREN.

[This is interesting as being probably the original of "Trouble of the world" (No. 10,) and peculiarly so from the following custom, which is described by a North Carolina negro as existing in South Carolina. When a *pater-familias* dies, his family assemble in the room where the coffin is, and, ranging themselves round the body in the order of age and relationship, sing this hymn, marching round and round. They also take the youngest and pass him first over and then under the coffin. Then two men take the coffin on their shoulders and carry it on the run to the grave.]

THE STORY

OF

JUBILEE SINGERS;

WITH THEIR SONGS.

BY

J. B. T. MARSH.

Revised Edition.

EIGHTY-FIFTH THOUSAND.

NEW YORK:
S. W. GREEN'S SON, 74 AND 76 BEEKMAN ST.
1883.

Ride on, King Jesus.

2 King Jesus rides on a milk-white horse,
No man can a hinder me;
The river of Jordan he did cross,
No man can a hinder me.
Cho.—Ride on, &c.

3 If you want to find your way to God,
No man can a hinder me;
The gospel highway must be trod,
No man can a hinder me.
Cho.—Ride on, &c.

What kind of shoes are you going to wear?

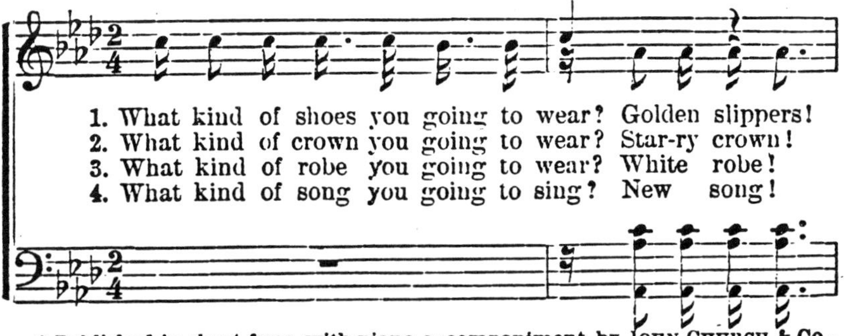

* Published in sheet form, with piano accompaniment, by John Church & Co., Cincinnati.

What kind of shoes you going to wear? Golden shlippers! Golden shlippers I'm
What kind of crown you going to wear? Starry crown ! Star-ry crown I'm
What kind of robe you going to wear? White robe ! Long white robe I'm
What kind of harp you going to play ? Golden harp ! Gold-en harp I'm
bound to wear, That out-shine the glit - ter - ing sun.
bound to wear, That out-shines the glit - ter - ing sun.
bound to wear, That out-shines the glit - ter - ing sun.
bound to play, That out-shines the glit - ter - ing sun.
Yes, yes,
Yes, yes, my Lord, I'm going to join the heavenly choir,
Yes, yes
Repeat pp
Yes, yes, yes, my Lord, I'm a sol - dier of the cross.

Inching along.

[Attention is called to the appropriateness of the melody for the expression of these singular words. It is all embraced within the first three tones of the scale, and thus may be said to be itself not more than an inch long.]

2 The Lord is coming to take us home,
Jesus will come by'nd-bye;
And then our work will soon be done,
Jesus will come by'nd-bye.

3 Trials and troubles are on the way,
Jesus will come by'nd-bye;
But we must watch and always pray,
Jesus will come by'nd-bye.

4 We'll inch and inch and inch along,
Jesus will come by'nd-bye;
And inch and inch till we get home,
Jesus will come by'nd-bye.

I ain't got weary yet.

2 Been praying for the mourner so long, &c.

3 Been going to the sitting-up so long, &c.

JUBILEE AND PLANTATION

CHARACTERISTIC FAVORITES,

As sung by the

HAMPTON STUDENTS, JUBILEE SINGERS, FISK UNIVERSITY STUDENTS, AND OTHER CONCERT COMPANIES.

Also, a Number of New and Pleasing Selections

.50

OLIVER DITSON COMPANY
THEODORE PRESSER CO., DISTRIBUTORS
1712 CHESTNUT STREET
• PHILADELPHIA •

O SINNER, YOU'D BETTER GET READY.

2 I heard of my Jesus a many one say—
Time is a-coming that sinner must die,
Could 'move poor sinner's sins away—
Time is a-coming that sinner must die.
Yes, I 'd rather a pray myself away—
Time is a-coming that sinner must die,
Than to lie in hell and burn a-one day,
Time is a-coming that sinner must die.
Cho.—O sinner, you'd better get ready, etc.

3 I think I heard a my mother say—
Time is a-coming that sinner must die,
'T was a pretty thing a to serve the Lord—
Time is a-coming that sinner must die.
Oh, when I get to Heaven I'll be able for to tell—
Time is a-coming that sinner must die,
Oh, how I shun that dismal hell—
Time is a-coming that sinner must die.
Cho.—O sinner, you 'd better get ready, etc.

RISE AND SHINE.

2 Oh, come on, mourners, get you ready, ready,
Come on, mourners, get you ready, ready, (*bis*,)
For the year of jubilee;
You may keep your lamps trimmed and burning, burning,
Keep your lamps trimmed and burning, burning, (*bis*,)
For the year of jubilee.
Cho.—Oh, rise and shine, etc.

3 Oh, come on, children, don't be weary, weary,
Come on, children, don't be weary, weary, (*bis*,)
For the year of jubilee;
Oh, don't you hear them bells a-ringing, ringing,
Don't you hear them bells a-ringing, ringing, (*bis*,)
For the year of jubilee.
Cho.—Oh, rise and shine, etc.

MUSIC

AND SOME

HIGHLY MUSICAL PEOPLE:

CONTAINING BRIEF CHAPTERS ON

I. A DESCRIPTION OF MUSIC. II. THE MUSIC OF NATURE.
III. A GLANCE AT THE HISTORY OF MUSIC.
IV. THE POWER, BEAUTY, AND
USES OF MUSIC.

FOLLOWING WHICH ARE GIVEN SKETCHES OF THE LIVES OF

REMARKABLE MUSICIANS OF THE COLORED RACE.

With Portraits,

AND AN APPENDIX CONTAINING COPIES OF MUSIC
COMPOSED BY COLORED MEN.

BY

JAMES M. TROTTER.

"A man should hear a little music, read a little poetry, and see a fine picture, every day of his life, in order that worldly cares may not obliterate the sense of the beautiful which God has implanted in the human soul." — GOETHE.

"'Tis thine to merit, mine to record." — HOMER.

FIFTH THOUSAND.

BOSTON:
LEE AND SHEPARD, PUBLISHERS.
NEW YORK:
CHARLES T. DILLINGHAM.
1881.

JOHNSON REPRINT CORPORATION JOHNSON REPRINT COMPANY LTD.
111 Fifth Avenue, New York, N.Y. 10003 Berkeley Square House, London, W. 1

MASS

FOR THREE VOICES.

GLORIA.

By SAMUEL SNAER, New Orleans.

De - o, glo - ri - a, glo - ri - a in ex - cel - sis
De - o, glo - ri - a, glo - ri - a in ex - cel - sis
De - o, glo - ri - a, glo - ri - a in ex - cel - sis

De - o.
p Solo.
De - o. Et in ter - ra pax ho-
p Solo.
De - o. Et in ter - ra pax ho - mi - ni-bus.

p Solo.
Et in ter - ra pax ho - mi - ni - bus,
- mi - ni - bus,

Tutti.
bo - næ vo-lun - ta - - tis,
Lau - da - mus
f
p
bo - næ vo-lun - ta - - tis,
Lau - da - mus
f
p
bo - næ vo-lun - ta - - tis,
Lau - da - mus
f
p

te, lauda - mus te, be - ne- di - ci- mus te, A - do - ramus
te, lauda - mus te, be - ne- di - ci- mus te, A - do - ramus
te, lauda - mus te, be - ne. di - ci- mus te, A - do - ramus

te, A-do - ramus te, glori-fi-camus te.
te, A-do - ramus te, glori-fi-camus te.
te, A-do - ramus te, glori-fi-camus te.
f

diminuendo.

1st Tenor. DUO.
Moderato.
dol.
Gra - ti - as a - gi - mus ti - bi, gra - ti - as
2d Tenor.
Gra - ti - as a - gi - mus ti - bi, gra - ti - as
Moderato.
p dol.

a - gi - mus ti - bi prop - ter mag-nam glo - ri - am
a - gi - mus ti - bi prop - ter mag-nam glo - ri - am

tu - am, Do - mi-ne De - us rex cœ - les - tis,
tu - am, Do - mi-ne De - us rex cœ - les - tis,
De - - - - - us pa - - - ter om - - - ni - po -
De - - - - - us pa - - - ter om - - - ni - po -
Allegretto.
- tens.
- tens.
Allegretto.
f

Do - mi - ne fi - - - - li u - ni - ge - ni -
Do - mi - ne.... fi - - - - li.... u - ni - ge - ni -
Do - mi - ne fi - - - - li u - ni - ge - ni -

- te,...... Je - - su Chri - ste, Je - su, Je - su
- te,...... Je - - su Chri - ste, Je - su, Je - su
- te, Je - - su Chri - ste, Je - su, Je - su

Chri-ste Do-mi-ne De-us, Ag-nus De-i
Chri-ste Do-mi-ne De-us, Ag-nus De-i
Chri-ste Do-mi-ne De-us, Ag-nus De-i

dim - in - uen - do.
fi-li-us pa-tris, Ag-nus De-i fi-li-us
fi-li-us pa-tris, Ag-nus De-i fi-li-us
fi-li-us pa-tris, Ag-nus De-i fi-li-us
dim - in - - uendo.

pa - tris.
pa - tris.
pa - tris.

Poco Andantino.
Solo. 1st Tenor.
pp
Qui tol - lis, qui tol - lis pec - ca - ta mun -
Poco Andantino.
pp
pp

- di, mi - se - re - re, mi - se - re - re, mi - se - re - re no - -

1st Tenor.
- bis.
2d Tenor.
DUO.
p
Qui tol - lis, qui tol - lis pec - ca - ta
Bass.
p
Qui tol - lis, qui tol - lis pec - ca - ta
p

mun - di, mi - se - re - re, mi - se - re - re no - - -
mun - di, mi - se - re - re, mi - se - re - re no - - -

p
Qui tol - lis, qui tol - lis pec - ca - ta mun -
- bis. Qui tol - lis, qui tol - lis pec - ca - ta mun -
- bis. Qui tol - lis, qui tol - lis pec - ca - ta
p

- di,.... sus - ci - pe, sus - ci - pe de - preca-ti - o - nem nos - -
- di,.... sus - ci - pe, sus - ci - pe de - preca-ti - o - nem nos - -
mun - di, sus - ci - pe, sus - ci - pe de - pre - ca-ti - o - nem nos - -
sf

1o. tempo.
- tram.
- tram.
- tram.
1o. tempo.
f
p SOLO. 2d Tenor.
Quo - niam tu so - - lus, sanctus tu so - lus Do - minus, ...
pp
tu...... so - lus al - - tis - - si - mus Je - su Chri ste.

1st Tenor.
Poco Allegro.
p
Cum sanc - to spi - ri - tu, cum sanc - to
2d Tenor.
p
Cum sanc - to spi - ri - tn, cum sanc - to
Bass.
p
Cum sanc - to spi - ri - tu, cum sanc - to
Poco Allegro.
p

cres - - cen - - do.
spi - ri - tu in glo - ri - a De - i pa - tris.
spi - ri - tu in glo - ri - a De - i pa - tris.
spi - ri - tu in glo - ri - a De - i pa - tris.
cres - cen - - do.

A - men, amen, a - men, a - men, a - men, a - men, a - meu,
A - men, amen, a - men, a - men, a - men, a - men, a - men,
A - men, amen, a - men, a - men, a - men, a - men, a - men,
f

a - meu, - men, a - men, a - men, a - men,
a - men, a - men, a - men, a - men, a - men,
a - men, a - men, a - men, a - meu, a - men,

f
A - men, amen, a - - - - men,
f
A - men, amen, a - - - - men,
f
A - men, amen, a - - - - men,
f
A - - - - men...............
A - - - - men...............
A - - - - men...............

5. The Nineteenth-Century Classical Tradition

The Fall of Zion

for Bass Voice and Orchestra

2.

10
whelm thee, Je-ru-sa-lem!
He shall rise in his an-ger

He shall rise and de-stroy thee,
dread hor-rors rise

3.
15
a2
on ev'ry side
the beau-ty of Is-rael shall per-ish, destruction waits up-
20
Aria Andantino
on her, the Lord will con-sume her in His an-ger.
O Je-

4.
25
ru-sa-lem what woes sur-round thee; dan — gers threat and
pp
30
fears con-found thee, O Je- ru-sa-lem! what woes sur-
p
I

5.
35
round thee; all a — round thee deep—'ning gloom.
40
45
cresc.
p
mf
fz
All — a-round — thee deep-'ning gloom. God's own thunders roll-ing

6.
50
cresc.
fz
o'er thee speak — His com — ing, speak thy doom. Speak His com-ing and speak thy
p
pizz.
arco
Allegro
55
pp
a2
doom. Hark! it is, it is the clar-ion's aw-ful sound bear-ing
f
pizz.
senza Vc.
tutti arco

7.
60
on the hol-low gales the shrill a-larms while the hills re-bel-low round to the
shock of hos-tile arms;
Loud-er yet the clang-ors rise;
a2
a1
cresc.

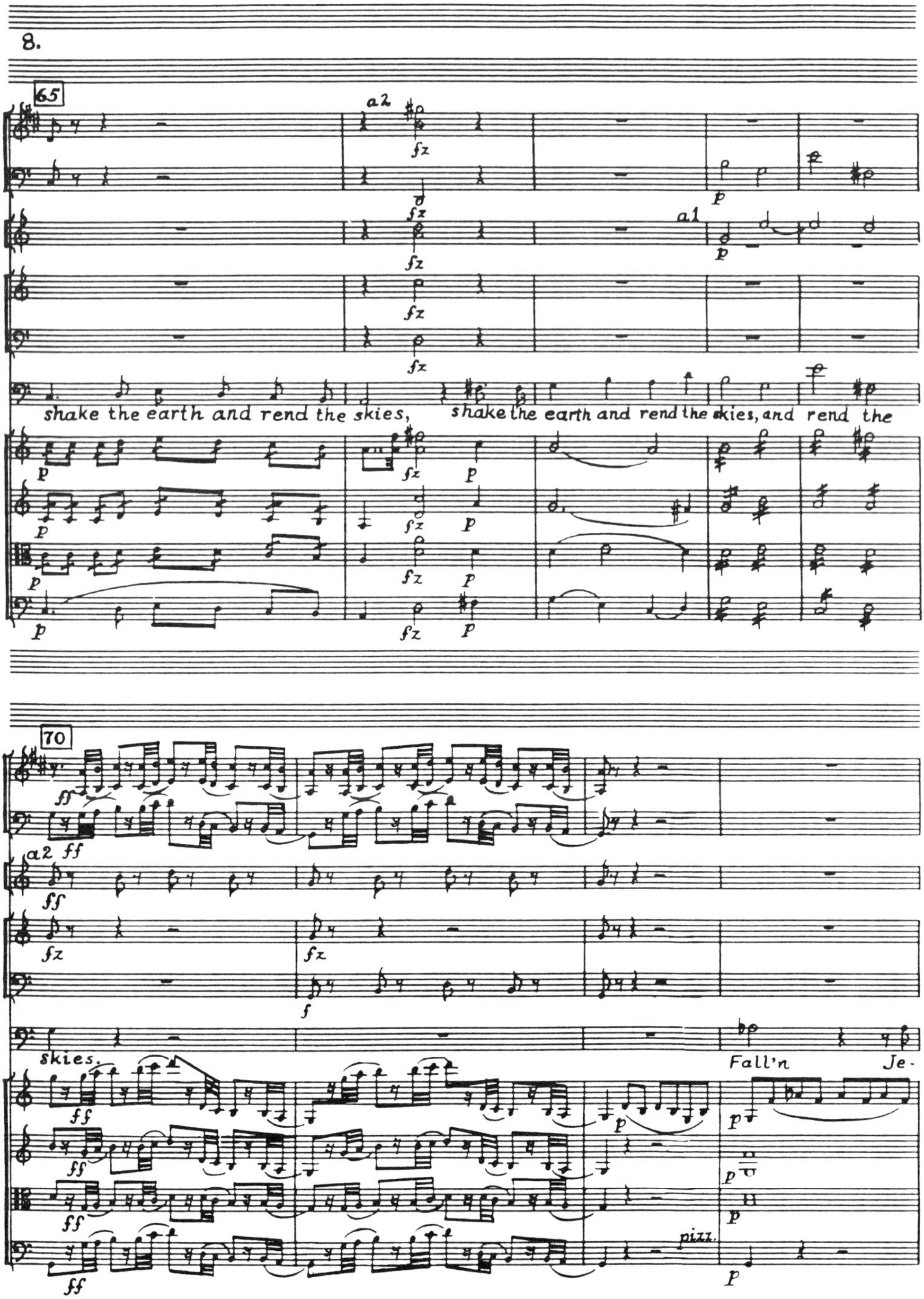

8.

65

a2

fz

p

a1

shake the earth and rend the skies, shake the earth and rend the skies, and rend the

9.
75
ru-sa-lem, fall'n Je – ru-sa-lem, hap-less land, the Lord hath spoken, thy
80
pow'r is broken, thy pow'r is broken to re-turn, ah, ne-ver

10.
85
A tempo
more, to re-turn, ah, ne-ver more. Loud and louder yet th'a-veng-ing an-gel
a2
fz
p
pizz.
senz Vc.
90
calls, see the battle on-ward bend its fiery course, like the
f
Tutti arco
arco

95
ff
fz
ff
fz
mount-tain tor-rent's force to-ward Sa-lem's bro-ken walls.
p
f
pp
fz
100
Hark! hark th'a-veng-ing an gel calls, he leads the fore-most
pizz.
arco
P
(p)

12.

105
band, fires ev' — 'ry heart, and strengthens ev' — ry
f
mf
p
pp
fz

110
hand. Hark! hark th'a-veng-ing a — gel calls, he leads the foremost
pizz.
arco
f
fz
p

I.
tutti
115
p cresc.
p cresc.
band; fires ev'ry heart and strengthens ev'ry hand.
cresc.
cresc.
cresc.
cresc.
f
f
f
f
f
f
f
f
120
fz
fz
fz
fz
fz
fz
fz
fz
fz

ST. PETER:

AN ORATORIO.

THE WORDS SELECTED FROM THE BIBLE,

AND THE MUSIC COMPOSED BY

JOHN KNOWLES PAINE.

BOSTON:
PUBLISHED BY OLIVER DITSON & COMPANY.
NEW YORK: C. H. DITSON & COMPANY.

ST. PETER.

Part I.

The Divine Call.

Introduction.

No. 1. *Chorus.*

The time is fulfilled, and the kingdom of heaven is at hand; repent, and believe the glad tidings of God.

Mark i. 15.

No. 2. *Recitative.* TENOR.

Now as Jesus walked by the sea of Galilee, he saw Simon and Andrew his brother casting a net into the sea. And he said unto them, Come ye after me, and I will make you fishers of men. And straightway they forsook their nets, and followed him.

Mark i. 16, 17, 18.

No. 3. *Air.* SOPRANO.

The spirit of the Lord is upon me; for he hath anointed me to preach good tidings to the poor; he hath sent me to bind up the broken hearted, to proclaim liberty to the captives, and to comfort all that mourn.

Isaiah lxi. 1, 2.

Recitative. TENOR.

And he called his twelve disciples together, and sent them out to preach the kingdom of God.

Luke ix. 1, 2.

No. 4. *Twelve Male Voices and Chorus.*

THE DISCIPLES AND BELIEVERS.

We go before the face of the Lord to prepare his ways, to give knowledge of salvation unto his people by the remission of their sins, through the tender mercy of our God; whereby the dayspring from on high hath visited us, to give light to them that sit in darkness and in the shadow of death, and to guide our feet in the way of peace.

Luke i. 76-79.

No. 5. *Choral.* *

How lovely shines the Morning Star!
The nations see and hail afar
The light in Judah shining.
Thou David's Son of Jacob's race,
My Bridegroom, and my King of grace,
For thee my heart is longing.
Lowly, holy,
Ever glorious and victorious is my Saviour;
He alone is King forever.

Schiedermann. Nicolai.

No. 6. *Recitative and Twelve Male Voices.*

SOPRANO.

And he asked his disciples, saying,

TENOR.

Who do men say that I am?

TWELVE DISCIPLES.

Some say that thou art John the Baptist; and others Elias, or one of the prophets.

TENOR.

But who say ye that I am?

SOPRANO.

And Simon Peter answered,

PETER. (Bass.)

Thou art the Christ, the Son of the living God.

Arioso. TENOR.

Blessed art thou, O Simon; for flesh and blood hath not revealed it unto thee, but my Father who is in heaven. And I say unto thee, that thou art Peter, and upon this rock will I build my church, and the gates of hell shall not prevail against it.

St. Matthew xvi. 16-18.

No. 7. *Air.* PETER. (Bass.)

My heart is glad, and my spirit rejoiceth; for thou wilt show me the path of life. In thy presence, O Lord, is fulness of joy; at thy right hand are pleasures forevermore.

Psalm xvi. 9-11.

No. 8. *Chorus.*

The Church is built upon the foundation of the apostles and prophets, Jesus Christ himself being the chief corner-stone. This is the Lord's doing; it is marvellous in our eyes.

Ephesians ii. 20. Psalm cxviii. 23.

The Denial and Repentance.

No. 9. *Recitative.* SOPRANO.

And when Jesus and his disciples had kept the passover, they went out to the Mount of Olives. And the Lord said,

Matthew xxvi. 30.

Arioso. TENOR.

Simon, Simon, behold! Satan hath desired to have you, that he may sift you as wheat. But I have prayed for thee, that thy faith fail not. And do thou, when thou hast returned to me, strengthen thy brethren.

PETER.

Lord, I am ready to go with thee both to prison and to death.

Luke xxii. 31-33.

Arioso. TENOR.

All ye shall be offended because of me this night.

PETER.

Though all men be offended, yet will I never be offended.

TENOR.

Verily I say unto thee, that this night before the cock crow, thou shalt deny me thrice.

PETER.

Though I should die with thee, yet will I not deny thee.

TWELVE DISCIPLES.

Though we should die with thee, yet will we not deny thee.

Matthew xxvi. 31-35.

* The *melodies* of the three Chorals contained in "St. Peter," have been selected from the Lutheran Choral Book, and arranged with original harmony and orchestration by the composer of the present work. This is in accordance with the custom among foreign composers of introducing into their sacred compositions the old, popular choral melodies, which are the peculiar offspring of a religious age. (For example, the melody of "Sleepers awake," in "St. Paul," was composed by Praetorious, 1604, being simply arranged and harmonised by Mendelssohn. This custom is further exemplified in "St. Paul," and in the Passions Music and Cantatas of Sebastian Bach.) It is deemed necessary to make this statement, in order to prevent any misapprehension that otherwise might arise as to the origin of these three melodies.

No. 10. *Air.* TENOR.

Let not your heart be troubled. Ye believe in God, believe also in me. In my Father's house are many mansions. I go to prepare a place for you; and I will come again and receive you to myself. Let not your heart be troubled, neither let it be afraid. My peace I give unto you.

St. John xiv. 1, 2, 3, 27.

No. 11. *Quartet and Chorus.*

Sanctify us through thy truth; thy word is truth.

St. John xvii. 17.

No. 12. *Recitative.* CONTRALTO.

And lo! Judas came with a great multitude, and they laid hold on Jesus, and led him away to the high-priest. Then all the disciples forsook him, and fled.

Matthew xxvi. 47, 50, 56, 57.

No. 13. *Chorus.*

We hid our faces from him; he was despised, and we esteemed him not. He was brought as a lamb to the slaughter, yet he opened not his mouth.

Isaiah liii. 3, 7.

No. 14. *Recitative and Chorus.*

CONTRALTO.

But Peter followed him afar off, even into the palace of the high-priest; and they that stood by said to him,

Soprano. MAID SERVANT.

Thou also wast with Jesus of Nazareth.

Bass. PETER.

I do not understand what thou sayest.

Chorus. THE SERVANTS.

Art not thou one of his disciples?

Tenor. MAN SERVANT.

This is one of them.

PETER.

I do not know the man.

Chorus. THE SERVANTS.

Surely thou art one of them; for thou art a Galilean; thy speech betrayeth thee.

PETER.

I know not this man of whom ye speak.

CONTRALTO.

And while he spake the cock crew. And the Lord turned and looked on Peter; and he remembered the word of the Lord; and he went out, and wept bitterly.

St. Matthew xxvi. St Mark xiv. St. Luke xxii. St. John xviii.

No. 15. *Lament.* (Orchestral.)

No. 16. *Air.* PETER. Bass.

O God, my God, forsake me not! Turn thee unto me, and have mercy upon me; for I am desolate and afflicted. O Lord, pardon mine iniquity, for it is great. O keep my soul, and deliver me.

Psalm xxv. 16, 11, 20.

No. 17. *Chorus of Angels.*

Remember from whence thou art fallen, and repent, and do the first works. And he that overcometh shall receive a crown of life.

Revelation ii. 5, 26, 10.

No. 18. *Air.* CONTRALTO.

The Lord is faithful and righteous to forgive our sins, if we walk in the light, as he is in the light.

1 John i. 9, 7.

No. 19. *Chorus.*

Awake, thou that sleepest; arise from the dead, and Christ shall give thee light. The darkness is past, and the true light now shineth.

Ephesians v. 14. 1 John ii, 8.

Part III.

The Ascension.

No. 20. *Chorus.*

The Son of Man was delivered into the hands of sinful men; he was crucified, and on the third day he rose again.

St. Luke xxiv. 7.

No. 21. *Choral.*

Jesus, my Redeemer, lives,
  Naught from him my soul can sever;
Bright the hope this promise gives,
  I with him shall live forever:
Shall I fear then? Can the head
Rise and leave the members dead?

Crüger. Louisa of Brandenburg.

No. 22. *Recitative and Solo.* TENOR & BASS.

After that he was risen from the dead, Jesus showed himself to his disciples. And none durst ask him, Who art thou? knowing that it was the Lord. And he saith to Peter, Simon, son of Jonas, lovest thou me more than these?

PETER.

Yea, Lord, thou knowest that I love thee.

TENOR.

Feed my lambs. Simon, lovest thou me?

PETER.

Yea, Lord, thou knowest that I love thee.

TENOR.

Feed my sheep. Simon, lovest thou me?

PETER.

Yea, Lord, thou knowest all things; thou knowest that I love thee.

TENOR.

Feed my sheep.

St. John xxi. 14-17.

Arioso. TENOR.

Go ye and teach all nations, baptizing them in the name of the Father, and of the Son, and of the Holy Ghost; teaching them to observe all things, whatever I have commanded you. And lo! I am with you always, even unto the end of the world.

St. Matthew xxviii. 19, 20.

No. 23. *Recitative.* SOPRANO.

And he lifted up his hands and blessed them. And it came to pass, while he blessed them, that he was parted from them and carried up to heaven.

St. Luke xxiv. 50, 51.

No. 24. *Chorus.*

If ye then be risen with Christ, seek those things which are above, where Christ sitteth on the right hand of God.

Colossians iii. 1.

Recitative. CONTRALTO.

And Peter, with the Eleven, went forth to preach, the Lord working with them.

St. Mark xvi. 20. Acts ii.

No. 25. *Air.* SOPRANO.

O man of God, be strong in the Lord, and in the power of his might. Put on the whole armor of God, and fight the good fight of faith, lay hold on eternal life, whereunto thou art called.

1 Timothy vi. 11, 12. Ephesians vi. 10, 11.

No. 26. *Quartet.*

Feed the flock of God, and when the chief shepherd shall appear thou wilt receive a crown of glory that fadeth not away.

1 Peter v. 2, 4.

Pentecost.

No. 27. *Recitative.* TENOR.

And when the day of Pentecost was come, the apostles were all together in one place. And suddenly there came a sound from heaven as of a rushing mighty wind; and it filled all the house where they were sitting; and there appeared unto them cloven tongues as of fire; and it sat upon each of them. And they were all filled with the Holy Ghost, and began to speak in other tongues, as the spirit gave them utterance.

Acts ii.

No. 28. *Chorus.*

The voice of the Lord divideth the flames of fire. The voice of the Lord is full of majesty, and every one doth speak of his glory.

Psalm xxix. 7, 4, 9.

Now when this was noised abroad the multitude came together; and they were amazed and marvelled, saying.

No. 29. *Chorus.*

Behold, are not all these who speak Galileans? and how is it that we every one hear them in our own tongue, wherein we were born? and how is it that we hear them speaking in our tongues the wonderful works of God?

Acts ii. 7, 8, 11.

Recitative. SOPRANO.

But Peter, standing up with the Eleven, lifted up his voice, and said unto them,

No. 30. *Air.* PETER. (BASS.)

Ye men of Judea, and ye that dwell at Jerusalem, hearken to my words. This is what was spoken by the prophet Joel, It shall come to pass in the last days, saith God, that I will pour out my spirit upon all flesh; and your sons and daughters shall prophesy, and your young men shall see visions, and your old men shall dream dreams. And I will show wonders in heaven above, and signs on the earth beneath, blood, and fire, and vapor of smoke; the sun shall be turned into darkness, and the moon into blood before the day of the Lord cometh, the great and notable day. And every one that calleth on the name of the Lord shall be saved.

Acts ii. 14-21. Joel ii. 28-32.

No. 31. *Air.* CONTRALTO.

As for man, his days are as grass; as a flower of the field, he flourisheth. For the wind passeth over it, and it is gone; and the place thereof shall know it no more. But the word of the Lord endureth forever; and this is the word which is preached to you.

Psalm ciii. 15, 16. 1 Peter i. 25.

No. 32. *Recitative.* PETER. (BASS.)

Ye men of Israel, hear these words! Jesus of Nazareth, a man approved of God to you, by miracles, and wonders, and signs, him ye have taken and by wicked hands, crucified and slain. This Jesus God raised up, whereof we all are witnesses. And being exalted by the right hand of God, and having received from the Father the promise of the Holy Ghost, he hath poured forth this, which ye now see and hear.

Acts ii. 22-33.

Recitative. TENOR.

Now when they heard this, they were pierced to the heart, and said unto Peter and the rest of the apostles,

No. 33. *Chorus.*

Men and brethren, what shall we do to be saved?

Acts ii. 37, 38.

No. 34. *Recitative and Twelve Male voices.*

PETER.

Repent, and be baptized every one of you in the name of Jesus Christ for the forgivness of sins, and ye shall receive the gift of the Holy Ghost. For the promise is to you and your children, and to all that are afar off, as many as the Lord our God shall call.

TWELVE DISCIPLES.

For the promise is to you and your children, and to all that are afar off, as many as the Lord our God shall call.

Acts ii. 38, 39.

Recitative. TENOR.

While Peter yet spake, the Holy Ghost fell on all that heard the word. And a great number believed, and were baptized, praising God.

Acts ii. 41, 47; x. 44.

No. 35. *Chorus.*

This is the witness of God which he hath testified of his Son. We know that the Son of God is come, and hath given us understanding that we may know the True One.

1 John v. 9, 20.

No. 36. *Choral.*

Praise to the Father,
  The glorious King of creation!
Bow down before him,
  Ye chosen of every nation!
  O, my soul, wake!
  Harp, lute and psaltery take,
Sound forth thy glad adoration!

Neander.

Recitative. SOPRANO.

And Peter said,

PETER.

Go and show these things to the brethren:

Acts xii. 17.

No. 37. *Solo and Chorus.*

PETER AND THE ELEVEN.

Now as ye were redeemed with the precious blood of Christ, love one another with a pure heart. And may the trial of your faith be found unto praise, honor and glory, receiving the salvation of your souls.

CHORUS.

Beloved, let us love one another; for love is of God.

1 Peter, i. 18, 19, 22, 7, 9. 1 John iv. 7.

Recitative.

Then they glorified God, saying,

No. 38. *Duet.* SOPRANO & TENOR.

Sing unto God, sing praises to his holy name, who called us out of darkness into his wonderful light.

Acts xi. 18. Psalm lxviii. 4. 1 Peter ii. 9.

No. 39. *Chorus.*

Great and marvellous are thy works, Lord God Almighty; just and true are thy ways, thou King of saints. All nations shall come and worship before thee, for thy judgments are made manifest. We praise thee, O Lord, and glorify thy name for evermore: Amen.

Revelation xv. 3, 4. Psalm lxxxvi. 12.

CONTENTS.

PART FIRST.

PART SECOND.

ST. PETER.

INTRODUCTION.

f
f
più f
ff sempre.
marcato.
decres
p
B.
pp e leggiero.
p dolce.
(Wind.)
(Strings.)
cres poco a poco.
mf poco a poco accel. e cres

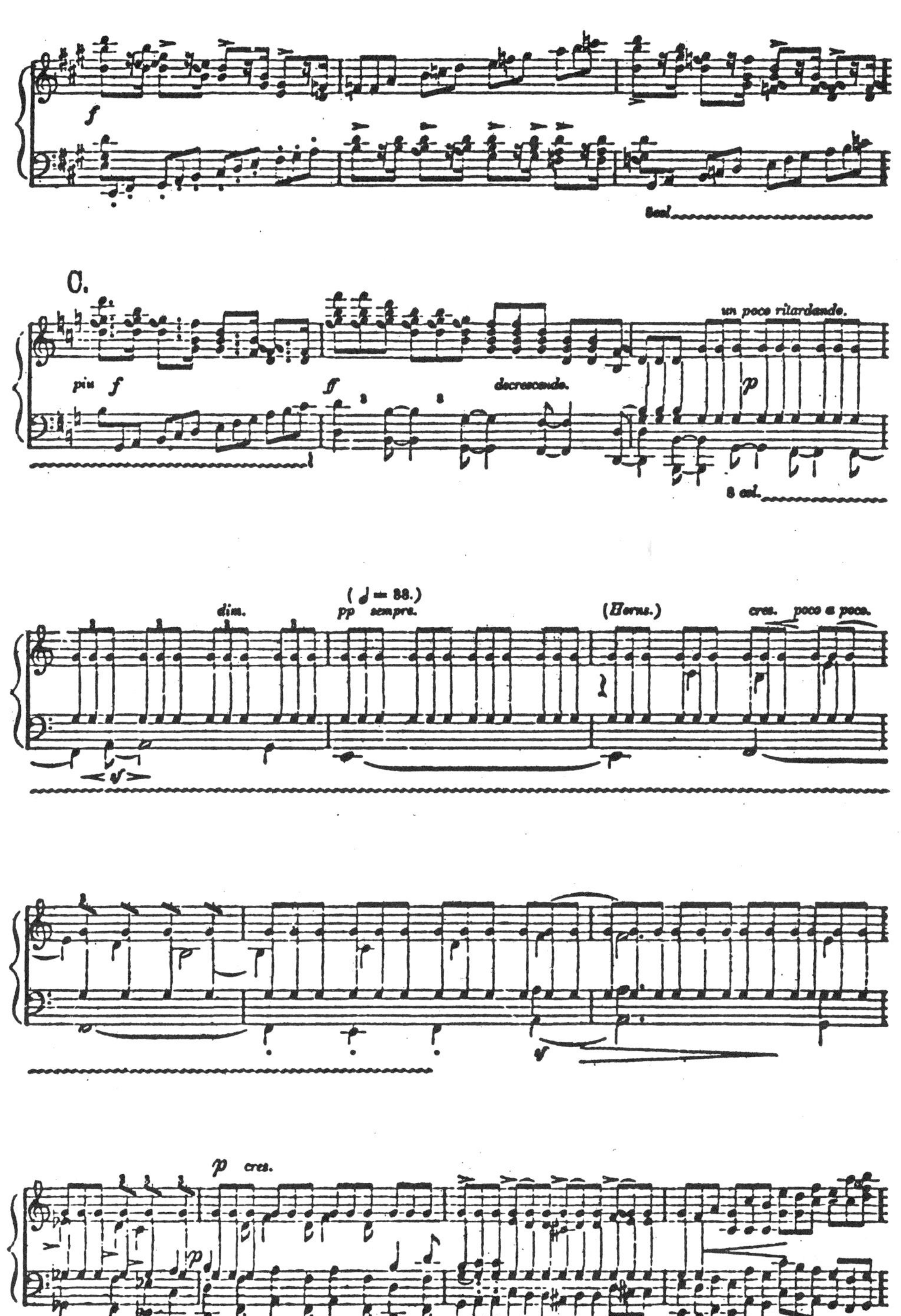

f
8va!
O.
più f
ff
decrescendo.
un poco ritardando.
p
8 col.
dim.
(𝅗𝅥 = 88.)
pp sempre.
(Horns.)
cres. poco a poco.
sf
sf
p cres.
p
8 col.

THE DIVINE CALL.

No. 1. CHORUS.—THE TIME IS FULFILLED.

D
hand,
hand,
the time is ful -
hand,
the time is ful - fill - - -
hand,
the time is ful -
mf
Ped.
8va
the time is fulfill'd, and the king - dom of heav - en is at
fill'd, and the king - dom of heav'n is at
ed, and the king - dom of heav'n is at
fill'd, and the king - dom of heav'n is at
cres.
f Ped.
E
ff ten.
hand;
hand;
re -
ff Ped.
decres.
p
mf

mf
re -
mf
re - pent, and believe the glad.... ti - - - - - dings of
pent, and be-lieve the glad ti - - dings, ti - - dings
mf
re - pent, and believe the glad ti - - dings of God, ...
pent, and be - lieve .... the glad.... ti - dings, glad .... ti - dings,
God, re -
of God,
re - pent,........ and be - lieve .... the glad .... ti - dings
of.... God,
pent,...... re - pent, and be - lieve the glad...............
f
re - pent, and be - - lieve,

F
glad ti-dings of God,
re-
ti - dings of God, re-pent, and be-lieve
re - pent, and believe the glad tidings of
re - pent, and be-lieve the glad ti - - -
pent, and be-lieve,
the glad
God, and be - lieve the glad ti - dings
G
dings, glad ti - dings of God.
believe the ti - dings of God.
ti - dings, glad ti - dings of God.
glad.... ti - dings of God.

the time is fulfill'd,
the time is ful -
poco a poco crescendo.
and the king - dom of heav'n is at hand,........ heav-en is at
and the king - - dom of heav'n is at hand,........ heav-en is.... at....
fill'd, and the king - dom, and the king - dom of heav'n is at
of heav - en is at
H
hand; re - pent,
hand; re-pent, and be -
hand; re - pent, and be-lieve, re - pent, re-pent,
hand; re - pent, and be-lieve........ re - pent, re-pent,

cresc.
and believe the glad ti - - - - dings of God,
cresc.
lieve the glad ti - - dings of God,
cresc.
and believe .... the glad.... ti - - dings of - God, be -
cresc.
and be-lieve.................................... be - lieve the
f
cresc.
mf
sf
be - lieve.... the glad ti - dings of
ff
be - - lieve.......... the glad
lieve the glad.... ti - dings, glad ti - dings of
ff
glad..................... ti - - dings, glad ti - dings of
sf
ffz
God,
God,
p
cresc.

I
the time is ful - fill'd, the time is ful-
the time is ful - fill'd, the time is fulfill'd, and the king-dom of heav-en is at hand,
the
fill'd, the king - dom of heav'n, the
and the king - - - - dom, the
and the king-dom of heav - - en is............ at hand,......
king - - - - dom of heav'n is at hand.
king - dom of heav - - en is at hand. . . ..
king - dom of heav-en is at hand, re-
J

pp
re - pent, and be - lieve the glad
pp
re - pent, and be-lieve the glad....
pp sempre.
re - pent, and be-lieve the glad.... ti - dings of God,
pent, and be - lieve, ... be - lieve
8va
K cres. poco a poco.
ti - dings, the glad ti - dings, the glad ti - dings,
ti - dings,
cres. poco a poco.
the glad ti - dings, the glad ti - dings, the glad
glad ti-dings of
cres. poco a poco.
f
re - pent, re - pent, re - pent, and be-lieve the glad ti - dings, the
cres
ti - dings of God, re - pent, re-pent, and be-lieve the glad ti - dings, the
God, re - pent, re - pent, re - pent, and be-lieve the glad ti - dings, the
8va
8va

ff sosten.
L
glad... ti - dings of God,
glad.... ti - - dings of God,
ff
glad ti - dings of God.
ff Sempre.
decres
be-lieve the glad ti - dings of God,
p
re-pent, and be-lieve,
pp
re-
pp
pp Rall al Fine.
glad ti-dings of God...........
pp dim.
Rall al Fine.
the glad ti-dings of God...............
be - lieve the glad ti-dings of God................
pent, the glad ti - - - - dings of God.... ....
Rall al Fine.
ppp

No. 2. Recit.—NOW AS JESUS WALKED BY THE SEA OF GALILEE.

No. 3. Air.—THE SPIRIT OF THE LORD IS UPON ME.

he...... hath sent me to bind up the bro - ken-heart - ed,
mf animato e cres
f
f
to pro-claim lib - er - ty, pro - claim lib - er - ty,
poco accel
cres.
fz
cres.
decres
ff
lib - er - ty to the cap - tives, and to com - fort all............ that mourn,
p
sf
ten.
ten.
N.
a tempo.
sosten.
the spir - - it of the
sf
sf dim.
dolce.
sf dim.
Lord is upon me, the spirit of the Lord is upon me; for he hath anointed
sf

me to preach good tidings to the poor; he hath sent me to bind up the bro - ken -
heart - ed, the broken-heart-ed, to pro - claim..........
lib - - - er-ty, lib - er-ty to the captives, and to comfort all that mourn,
he hath sent me to com - fort all that mourn.
RECIT.—AND HE CALLED HIS TWELVE DISCIPLES TOGETHER.
TENOR VOICE. Recit.
And he called his twelve disciples together, and sent them out to preach the kingdom of God.

No. 4. Twelve Male Voices and Chorus.—WE GO BEFORE THE FACE OF THE LORD.

P
by the re - mis - sion
by the re - mis - sion of their sins, ... the re - mis - sion of their sins, thro' the
cres.
sf
dim.
ten - der mer - cy of our God, the ten - der mer - cy of our God.
p
cresc.
sf dim. e Ritard.
G A tempo.
CHORUS
We
CHORUS.
CHORUS.
We
CHORUS.
A tempo.
mf
p

go be - fore the face of the Lord to pre - pare his ways, pre -
go be - fore the face of the Lord to pre - pare his ways, pre -
pare his ways, to give.... know - ledge of.... sal -
pare his ways, to give, to give, to give.... know - ledge of.... sal -
cres.
R
va - tion un - to his peo - ple by the re - mis - sion of their
va - tion un - to his peo - ple by the re - mis - sion of their
by the re - mis -

sins, by the re - mis - sion of their sins, thro' the
sins, by the re - mis - sion of their sins,........
sion, by the re - mis - sion of their sins,
cres. f dim.
ten - der mer - cy of .... our God, the ten - der mer - cy
p cres f dim.
through the mer - cy of our God, the ten - der mer - cy
cresc. dim.
cres f sf dim. sf
S
of our God;
of our God;
TWELVE DISCIPLES.
TENORS. mf sostenuto.
Chorus tacet.
where - by the
BASSES. mf sostenuto.
sf

Unison
day - spring from on high hath vis - it-ed us, to give
sf
T
cres
light, give light to them that sit .... in dark - ness
cres
SOPRANO CHORUS.
mp
whereby the day - spring from on....
ALTO CHORUS.
p
sf
and in the shadow of death, and in the shad-ow of death,
8va

dim.
pp
p
high hath vis - it-ed us to give light to them that sit in
and to guide our feet in the way of peace,
U
sf
dark - ness, and in the shadow of death, and to guide our feet
to guide our feet,
and to guide our feet
V
A tempo.
in the way of peace, where -
in the way of peace, where
TENOR CHORUS.
BASS CHORUS.
Ritard.
pp (Horn.)

by the day-spring from on high hath vis-it-ed us, hath
by the day-spring from on high hath vis-it-ed us, hath
vis-it-ed us, to give.... light to them that sit in
cres.
vis-it-ed us, to give.... light........ to them that sit in
to give light
p
cres
sf
dim.
W p
dark-ness and in the shad-ow of death, and to
mf
and to guide, and to guide our feet,
dark-ness and in the shad-ow of death, and to guide, to guide our
12 MALE VOICES.
fz
sf

p ritard. pp
guide............ our feet in the way of peace,
dim e ritard. pp
and to guide our feet in the way of peace, the way of peace,
CHORUS. p dim e ritard. pp
feet to guide our feet in the way, the way of peace,
CHORUS. mf dim e ritard.
in the way of peace,
p dim e ritard. pp
X
mf
and to guide, to guide our feet in the
mf
12 MALE VOICES.
CHORUS.
and to guide our feet, and to guide, to guide our feet in the
CHORUS.
guide.......... our feet in the
mf
8va
Sempre legato.
dim. pp
way of peace.....................
dim. pp
dim. pp
way of peace.....................
dim. pp
rall
p dim. pp dim.
ppp

No. 5. CHORAL.—HOW LOVELY SHINES THE MORNING STAR.

No. 6. Solo and 12 Male Voices.—AND HE ASKED HIS DISCIPLES.

TENOR ARIOSO.
Son of the liv - ing God. Bless - ed art thou, O Si - mon, for
Con moto.
dolce.
p
flesh and blood hath not re-veal'd it un - to thee, but my
dim.
poco piu moto e agitato.
Fa - ther who is in heav - en. And I say un - to
poco piu moto.
sf
Rit.
thee that thou art Pe - ter, and upon this rock will I build my
ff
church, and the gates of hell shall not pre-vail against it.
A tempo.
sf
p

No. 7. AIR.—MY HEART IS GLAD.

path.................. of life:............
A
ff
decres.
in thy pres-ence, O Lord, is ful-ness of
dim.
p
poco a poco. cres.
joy,.... at thy..... right hand, are pleas - - -
pp cres.
- ures, are pleas-ures for ev - er - more,....
B
in thy
cres.
f
dim.
p
pres-ence is ful - ness of joy,............... at thy right hand are
cres.
fz
fz
f

pleas - - ures, are pleas - ures for ev - - er -
more,
My heart is glad and my
dim.
p
spir - it re - joic - eth, for thou wilt show me the path of.... life: in thy
Rall.
tempo.
pres - ence, O Lord, is ful - ness of joy,.... in

thy............ pres - ence is ful - ness of joy,.... at thy ....
dim.
...... right hand.... are pleas - ures for ev - - - - - er - more, at
dim. p.
f
f
dim.
8va
ad lib.
thy right hand .... are pleasures for ev - er, for ev - er -
f
more.
A tempo.
cres.
fz
p
dim.
Ped.
pp
dim.
ppp

No. 8. Chorus.—THE CHURCH IS BUILT.
Maestoso. ♩ = 100.
Soprano.
Alto.
Tenor.
Bass.
Accomp.
The Church is built up - on the foun - da - tion
The Church is built up - on the foun - da - tion
marcato.
of the a - pos - tles and prophets, Jesus Christ himself being the chief corner - stone, ...
chief cor - - ner -
of the a - pos - tles and prophets, Je - sus Christ himself being the chief . . . . cor - ner -
chief corner - stone . . . .
cres.
dim.
D
. . . . the Church is built up - on the foun - da - tion of the apostles and prophets,
stone, the Church is
stone, the Church - is built up - on the foun - da - tion of the apostles and prophets,
cres.

pp
ten.
Je - sus Christ him - self being the chief corner-stone.
Je - - sus Christ
Je - - sus Christ himself being the chief corner-stone.
Je - - sus Christ
dim e rall.
Allegro Maestoso. ♩ = 120.
This is the Lord's do - ing, this is the Lord's do - ing, it is
This is the Lord's do - ing, the Lord's
This is the Lord's do - ing,
Allegro Maestoso.
marcato.
mar - vel - lous in our eyes,
it is mar - vel - lous in our eyes,
do - ing,
this is the Lord's do - ing, it is mar - vel - lous in our

E
this is the Lord's do - ing,
this is the Lord's do - ing,
eyes, this is the Lord's do - ing, it is
it is mar - vel -
mar - vel - lous
lous in our eyes,
F A tempo.
this is the Lord's do - ing, the Lord's do - ing,
in our eyes, this is the Lord's do - ing, this is the Lord's
ritard.
A tempo.

G
the Lord's do - ing, this is the Lord's
'tis mar - vel-lous in our eyes, this
it is mar - vel - lous in our eyes,
do - - ing, it is mar - vel - lous in our eyes,
cres. poco a poco.
do - ing, this is the Lord's do - ing, it is
is the Lord's.......... do - ing, it is
this is the Lord's do - ing, 'tis
this is the Lord's do - - - - -
tr tr tr tr
p
mar - vel - lous in our eyes, 'tis mar - vel - lous in our eyes,
mar - vel - lous, mar - vel - lous in our eyes,
mar - - vel - lous............. in our eyes,
ing, 'tis mar - - - vel - lous in our eyes,
ff
f
fz

in our eyes,
in our eyes,
decres.
Tempo primo Maestoso.
The Church is
The Church is
ten.
Tempo primo Maestoso.
p
dim.
ten.
ten.
cres.
f
8col.
built up-on the foun - da - tion of the a - pos - tles and prophets, Jesus Christ him-
built up-on the foun - da - tion of the a - pos - tles and prophets, Jesus Christ him-
ff

sf
rit poco.
ten.
self being the chief corner - stone,............
chief cor - - ner - stone.
self being the chief .... cor - ner - stone.
chief corner - stone..........
rit poco.
dim. e
Rall.
Allegro maestoso.
the Lord's
This is the Lord's do - ing, this is the Lord's do - ing, 'tis
This is the Lord's do - ing, it is
This is the Lord's do - ing, it is mar -
Allegro maestoso.
tr
H
do - ing, 'tis mar - vel - lous in our eyes, it is mar -
mar - vel - lous in our eyes, in our eyes,
mar - vel - lous in our eyes, this is the Lord's
.... vel - lous in our eyes,

vel - lous.......... in
this is the Lord's do - ing, it is mar- - - vel-lous in our
do - ing, 'tis marvellous in our
this is the Lord's do - ing, it is mar -vel - lous
tr tr
I
rall poco a poco al fine.
our eyes, this is the Lord's do - ing, 'tis
eyes,......................
rall poco a poco al fine.
eyes,...................... this is the Lord's do - ing, it is
in our eyes,
sf sf sf rall poco a poco al fine.
ff sosten.
mar - vel - lous in .... our eyes.........
ff
mar - - vel - lous in our eyes........
ff sosten.
mar - vel - lous in........ our.... eyes.........
ff sosten.
mar - - - vel - lous in our eyes.........
ff
sostenuto.

THE DENIAL AND REPENTANCE.

No. 9. Recit. and Arioso.—AND WHEN JESUS AND HIS DISCIPLES.

più mosso e agitato.
cres.
f
thou, when thou hast return'd to me, strengthen thy brethren.
cres.
dim.
f
p
Peter. Recit.
dim.
Grave.
p
Lord, I am read-y to go with thee, both to pris - on and to death.
p
dim.
pp
Solo and Twelve Male Voices.—ALL YE SHALL BE OFFENDED.
Tenor Solo.
Allegro moderato. ♩ = 100.
All ye shall be of-fend - ed be-cause of me this night.
p
sf
Peter.
Though all men be of-fend - ed, yet will I nev - er be of - fend - ed.
Oboe.
p
Tenor Solo.
Ver - i - ly I say unto thee, that this night before the
espress.
rit poco.
mf
cres.

No. 10. AIR.—LET NOT YOUR HEART BE TROUBLED.

Andante con moto. ♩ = 69.

TENOR SOLO.

ACCOMP.

sf > *p dolce.*

dolce.

poco rit.
dim.
pp
With feeling.
Let not your heart, ... your heart........ be troub - led,
p
let not your heart, ... your heart be troub - -
dim.
dim.
led; ye believe in God, ye believe in God, be -
ritard.
cres.
cres.
p
f
ritard.
dim.
lieve al - so in me, believe al - so in me.
A tempo.
dim.
p
ten.
ten.
ten.
cres.
ten.
f

L
In my Fa - ther's house are ma - ny man - sions,
in my Fa-ther's house are man-y man - sions, are many man - sions.
pp
sf
f
I go to prepare a place for you, I go to prepare a place for you;
dim.
p
ritard.
ad lib.
A tempo.
and I will come again, and re-ceive you to my-self,...... and re -
ceive you to myself.
ritard.
A tempo.
cantando.

mf
dim.
rit.
pp
Let not your heart.......... your heart.......... be troub - led,
animato.
let not your heart, your heart be troub - led, neither let it be
sf
f
rit poco e dim.
afraid, let not your heart.... be troubled, neither let it be afraid. My
f
dim.
p
A tempo.
peace I give un - - to you.
p
rit.
p
dim.
pp

No. 11. Quartet and Chorus.—SANCTIFY US THROUGH THY TRUTH.

M CHORUS.
CHORUS.
Thy word is
CHORUS.
Thy word is
CHORUS.
Thy word.... is truth, thy
fz
fz
Poco piu mosso, ♩. = 58.
Thy word.... is truth, sanc - - ti -
truth, thy word is truth,
truth.... is truth, sanc - - ti -
word.... is truth,
Poco piu mosso.
sf pp cres. poco a poco.
fy us through thy
fy us through thy
through...... thy
sf
sf
f

dim.
pp
cres. poco a poco.
truth; .... thy .... word is
dim.
pp
cres. poco a poco.
dim.
pp
cres. poco a poco.
truth; .... thy .... word is
dim.
pp
cres. poco a poco.
sf dim.
ppp
cres. poco a poco.
accel.
truth, thy word is
accel.
truth, thy word is
accel.
sf
ff
truth, ...
ff
ff
truth, ...
ff
ff sostenuto.
decres.

Rall molto.
N Contralto Solo.
Sanc - ti - fy - us, sanc - ti-fy us through thy truth,
Tempo primo.
Soprano Solo.
sanc - - ti - fy us, sanc - ti - fy us thro' thy truth;
Alto Solo.
sanc-ti - fy us thro' thy truth;
Tenor Solo.
sanc - - ti - fy us, sancti - fy us, sanc - ti - fy us
Bass Solo.
us thro' thy truth;
dim.
sanc - - ti - fy us, sanc - - ti - fy us
sanc - ti - fy us, sanc - ti - fy us through thy truth,
sanc - ti - fy us through thy truth, through thy truth,

Soprano Solo.
through thy truth; sanc-ti-fy us through thy truth; thy word is truth....
CHORUS.
pp sempre.
thy word is truth,.......... is truth,
SOLO. mf
thy word is
thy word is truth,... .... is truth, thy word is
SOLO.
thy
pp sempre.
thy word is truth, sanc- ti-fy us through thy truth, thy word is truth.
thy .... word, thy word is truth.
truth............
truth,... ... . thy...... word....... .... is truth.
word is truth, thy word is truth, thy word is truth.
dolce.
sf
wind ins
p
ritard.
dim.
pp

No. 12. Recit.—AND LO! JUDAS CAME WITH A GREAT MULTITUDE.

No. 13. Chorus.—We hid our faces from him.
Andante patetico. ♩ = 72.
Soprano.
Alto.
Tenor.
Bass.
Accomp.
Andante patetico.
We hid our fa - ces
We hid our fa - ces from him, our fa - ces from
We hid our fa - ces from him, from
We hid our fa - ces from him; he was des-pis-ed, des-pis-ed, and we es-
from him;
him; he was des-pis-ed, des-pis-ed, and we es-
dim.
teem'd him not, and we esteem'd him not.
and we es-teem'd him not.
teem'd him not, and we es - teem-ed him not.
sf
Allegro. ♩ = 120.
Allegro.
pp cres.

mf
He was brought as a lamb to the slaugh -
sf
He was brought as a lamb to the slaugh -
He was brought as a lamb,
mf
dim.
ter, he was brought as a lamb to the slaugh - ter,
mf
ter, he was brought as a lamb to the slaugh - ter,
cres.
Dim
R
riten.
yet he o-pen'd not his mouth, he open'd not his mouth,
p
yet he o-pen'd not his mouth, he open'd not his mouth,
p dolce.
(Oboe.)
p
riten.

S Andante primo.
we hid our fa-ces from him;
we
we hid our fa-ces
Andante primo.
rall.
p
he was despised, and we es-teem - - - ed him
hid our fa-ces from him;
from him; he was despis-ed, he was despis'd,
we hid our fa - ces from him; he was des-pis-ed, and we
dim. T Allegro.
not.
He was brought as a
and we es-teem'd him not.
He was brought as a
and we esteem'd him not.
He was brought as a
.... es - teem'd him not.
Allegro. = 120.
dim.
p cres.
f

dim.
lamb, ... brought to the slaugh - ter, yet he
dim.
dim.
lamb, brought to the slaugh - ter, yet he
dim.
dim.
Andante. A tempo.
p
o-pen'd not his mouth, he o - pen'd not his mouth. . . . .
pp
p
pp
o-pen'd not his mouth, he o - pen'd not his mouth. . . . .
pp
Andante. A tempo. Allegro.
p
pp
cres.
Meno Allegro.
f
fz
dim.
pp
ppp

No. 14. RECIT. WITH CHORUS.— BUT PETER FOLLOWED HIM.

U Chorus. The Servants.
ff Allegro con fuoco.
Art not thou one of his disciples? art not thou one of his dis-ci-ples?
Art not thou one of his disciples? art not thou one of his dis-ci-ples?
Art not thou one of his disciples? art not thou one of his, of his dis-ci-ples?
Tenor Solo. Servant.
f. sostenuto.
This is one of them.
mp cres.
fz
Peter
I do not know the man.
V Chorus. Allegro di molto.
Sure-ly thou art one of them,
Sure-ly thou art one of them, sure-ly thou art one of them, one of them,
Sure-ly thou art, sure-ly thou art one of them, sure-ly thou art one of them, one of them,
Sure-ly thou art one of them, sure-ly, sure-ly thou art
Allegro di molto. 𝅗𝅥 = 96.

ff
one of them; for thou art a Gal - i - le - an, thy speech be -
ff
ff
one of them; for thou art a Gal - i - le - an, thy speech be -
ff
f
W
tray-eth thee,
surely thou art one of them,
tray-eth thee,
sure-ly thou art one of them, sure-ly thou art
p cres. mf
sure - ly thou art one of them, one of them; for
sure - ly thou art one of them, thou art one of them; for
one of them, thou art one of them; for
sure - - - ly, sure-ly thou art one of them; for
ff

ff
thou art a Gal-i-le-an, thy speech be-tray-eth thee......
thou art a Gal-i-le-an, thy speech be-tray-eth thee......
Recit. Peter.
I know not this man of whom ye speak.
Grave.
Contralto Recit.
(Horns.)
sf p
ffz
And while he yet spake, the cock crew. And the Lord turn-ed and look-ed on Pe-ter; and he remember'd the word of the Lord: and he went out, and wept bit-ter-ly.
with feeling.
col voce.
pp

LAMENT.

No. 15.

Adagio con gran espressione e agitato. ♩=66.
Orchestra. pp
sf
sf
sf
pp
sf
accel e cres.
sf
tempo primo.
f
cres.
Ped.
Ped.
Ped.
Ped.
Ped.
f
poco piu mosso. ♩ = 80.
X
ff
ffz
p
fz

Y
ff
Dim.
p
ppp
con sordino.
espress.
sf
cres.
Tempo primo.
mf cantando.
sf
cresc. sempre
8va
ff
decres.
mp
dim.
Lento.
ritard.
attacca.
pp

No. 16.
AIR.—O GOD, MY GOD, FORSAKE ME NOT!
Andante appassionata. ♩ = 72.
PETER.
BASS SOLO.
ACCOMP.
O God, my God, forsake me not! Turn thee un-to me, turn thee un-to me, and have mer - - cy up-on me, have mer - cy up - on me; for I am des-o-late and af - flict - ed,
for I am des-o-late and af-flict - ed.
O Lord,
pp
cres.
mf
p
cres.
sf
ten.
ten.
p
poco. ritard.
ad lib.
A Piu mosso e agitato. ♩ = 92.
sf
p
sf
sf cres.

riten.
tempo.
pardon mine in - i - qui-ty; for it is........ great,
sf f sf sf riten. tempo. dim.
sf
rit.
O Lord, pardon mine ini -qui - ty; for it is great,.... is
p sf Dim. rit.
B
great, O par - don mine in - i-qui-ty; for it is great.
a tempo cres. f
O keep my soul, and de - liv - er me, O keep my
sf
poco rit.
soul, and deliv - er me,
ritard.
dim. dim. p dim. pp

Tempo primo.
pp
cres.
O God, my
rit.
God, forsake me not!
Turn thee un-to me, turn thee
mf
p
un-to me, and have mer - cy up-on me, have mer - cy up -
on me;
for I am des-o-late and af-flict-ed,
poco ritard.
for I am
sf
ten.
ten.
C Piu mosso e agitato.
des-o-late and af-flict - ed.
O
p
p
sf
p
sf

Lord, pardon mine in - i - qui - ty, O par - don mine in -
i - qui -ty; for it is great.
O keep my soul, and de - liv - er me, O keep my soul, and de -
liv - er me, O God, for -sake me not, O
God, for - sake me not, my God, for - sake me not.
sf
f
cres.
decres.
8va
Rallentando
Dim.
p
A tempo.
Ritard. molto.
pp

No. 17. Chorus of Angels.—REMEMBER FROM WHENCE THOU ART FALLEN.
(To be sung by a small chorus of select voices.)
Moderato e tranquillo.
1st. Soprano.
2nd. Soprano.
1st. Contralto.
2nd. Contralto.
Accomp.
Re - mem - ber, re - mem - ber from whence thou art fal - len,
remem - ber, re-mem - ber from whence thou art fal - len,
(Harp)
Ped.
R.H.
L.H.
D
and repent, re - pent, and do the first

dim.
poco rit.
works, repent, and do the first works, the first works.
works, repent, and do the first works.
Dim.
Ped.
Allegro. ♩= 120.
FULL CHORUS. Soprano.
And he that o - ver - cometh shall re -
Alto. mf animato.
And he that over-cometh, he shall receive a crown, re -
Tenor. mf animato.
And he that o-vercometh shall receive a crown of life, a
Bass.
Allegro.
sempre legato.
E
dolce.
ceive a crown of life, and he that o - ver - com - eth,
and
crown of life, and he that o - ver - com - eth,

mf cres.
and he that o - ver - com - eth shall re -
cres.
he that o - ver - com - eth, he shall re - ceive a
cres.
he shall re - ceive a
cres.
he that o - ver - com - eth,
8va.
F p
ceive a crown of life,
crown of life, he shall re - ceive a crown of life, re -
crown of life, he shall re - ceive a crown of life, re -
p Ped. * Ped. * Ped. Ped. Ped.
he shall re - ceive a crown of
ceive a crown of life,
ceive a crown of life,
he shall re - ceive a crown of
Ped Ped. Ped. Ped * f Ped.

SELECT VOICES.
Soprano 1st.
life,
re-pent, re-pent,
Soprano 2nd.
Contralto 1st.
life,
re-pent, re-pent,
Contralto 2nd.
Ped.
dim.
pp
p
FULL CHORUS.
Soprano.
cres.
re-pent, and do the first works.
Alto.
Tenor.
re-pent, and do the first works. And he that o - ver -
Bass.
mf cres.
And he that o - ver - com - eth shall re - ceive .... a
com - eth, and he that o - ver - com - eth shall re - ceive a
f

dim.
p
I
crown of life.... re-ceive a crown of life, and
dim.
p
crown........ of life.... re-ceive a crown of life, and
dim.
p
crown.... of life, shall re- ceive a crown of life,.......
dim.
p
crown,.................... a crown of life,
dim.
p
Cres. poco a poco.
ff
dim e ritard.
he that o- ver-com-eth shall re-ceive a crown, .. a crown.......
crown of life, re-ceive a
mp cres.
ff
and he that o- ver-com-eth shall re- ceive a crown, a
cres.
ff
dim e ritard.
re- ceive a crown, a crown
cresc. poco a poco.
ff
dim e ritard.
A tempo. dim.
.... of life..................................
A tempo.
crown of life..................................
A tempo. dim.
crown of life..................................
of life..................................
A tempo.
p
Ped.
dim.
poco rit.
pp
*

No. 18. AIR.—THE LORD IS FAITHFUL.

K
♩ = 96.
più mosso e energico.
give our sins, if we
rit.
ff
dim.
walk in the light,.... if we walk in the light,.... as
f
ff
p
dim.
ritard.
a tempo....
he.... is in the light, as he is in the light,
cres.
dim.
ritard.
p
Dimin.
L
Tempo primo. ♩ = 80.
The Lord is faith-ful and right-eous
pp
to for-give our sins, the Lord is faith-ful and right-eous,
p
mf

dim.
pp
M Piu mosso e energico.
faith - ful and right - eous to for-give our sins, if we
dim.
pp
sf
walk in the light, if we walk in the light, as he is in the
fz
più forte.
meno mosso.
dim.
light, the Lord is faith - ful and right - eous to forgive, ... to forgive our
mf
f sosten.
m.v.
ritard.
sins, ... if we walk in the light as he is in the
marcato.
ffz
A tempo.
light.
ritard molto.
dolce e dim.
Violino Solo.

No. 19. Chorus.—AWAKE, THOU THAT SLEEPEST.

N
rise from the dead, and Christ shall give thee light...
rise from the dead, and Christ shall give thee light...
The darkness is past and the
The darkness is past and the true light now shineth; a - wake, and
and Christ shall give thee light,
O
The darkness is
true light now shi - neth, now shi - - - - neth: a -
Christ shall give thee light, shall.. give.... thee..... light,
and Christ shall give........ thee light,

past and the true light now shi - neth, the dark - ness is past........ the true
wake, and Christ shall give thee light, ... a-wake, and Christ....
the true.. light.... now........ shi -
light... ...... now shi - - - neth, the true light now shi -
.... shall give.... thee.... light, the true light now shi -
- - - - - - neth, the
the darkness is past and the true light now shi - - - - neth, the
cres.
f
ff
- - - - neth,........ a - wake...
true light now shi - neth, ... a - wake....
P
decres.
p

dim.
pp
mf
... thou that sleep - - est, the dark - ness is past and the
the dark - - - -
.... thou that sleep - - est, the
cres.
true... ..... light.... ...... now shi - - - neth,
ness is past, and.... the true......
dark - - - - - ness is..... past, the dark - - - - ness is
the
the dark-ness is past, ... a -
light now shi - - - - - - - - - - neth, a - -
past, the dark - - - - ness is past, a - -
dark-ness is past and the true........ light now shi - - neth, a -
sf

dim.
p
pp
wake........
thou
that
sleep
f
wake.........
Q
est,
a - - - rise....
mp
a - - - rise............ a - -
marcato.
pp
cres.
mf
a - - rise from the dead, and Christ shall give.........
rise,.....................
from.... the.... dead,
a - - rise,..............
rise........ from the dead,

thee light, and Christ
rise from the dead
and Christ shall
and Christ shall give thee
mf
shall give thee light,
a
give thee light,
and Christ shall give
a - rise from the dead,
and Christ shall give
light, shall give thee light,
Christ
f
ff
decres.
-wake, a - wake, thou that
thee light, a wake, thou that sleep
shall give thee light
dim.
pp

poco rit.
R a tempo.
sleep - - - - - est,
The dark - - ness is past, and the
est,
a - wake, and Christ shall
cres.
true light.... .... now shi - - - neth,
and Christ shall give thee light, the darkness is
give thee light,.... ......
The dark - - - - ness is past and the true light now shi - -
the true .... light now shi - -
past and the true light now shi - neth, the true light now shi......
a - wake,....
- neth, a - - wake, and Christ shall give thee light, a -
mf
dim.
f
p

S
mf
dim.
p
-neth, a - - wake, ... thou that
mf
dim.
p
-neth, a - wake, ... thou that sleep - - - - - -
dim.
p
.... a - - wake .... thou .. that sleep - - - - - est, ...
dim.
p
- - wake, ... thou ... that ... sleep - - - - - - - - -
cres.
mf
dim.
p
dim.
sleep - - est, a - - rise from the dead, ...
dim.
p
..... est, a - - rise .... a -
dim.
p
..... a - rise .... a - - -
p
- - est, a - - rise from the dead ...
cres.
dim.
p
T
dim.
pp
- - rise from the dead, ... and Christ shall
dim.
pp
- - - - - - rise, ... and Christ shall
pp
...... a - - rise from the dead, ...
dim.
pp sempre

pp
cres.
and Christ shall give thee, give thee....
give........ thee,........... give thee
give.......... thee light, shall give thee
.... and Christ
U
ff
mf
light .... The
light............. The darkness is past and the true light now shi -
light.......... The dark-ness is past and the true light now shi -
light.... ..... a - - wake, and Christ shall
sf
f
darkness is past and the true light now shi - - - - - - - - - - - - - - neth,....
- neth, the true light, the true light now shi - neth,
. neth, now shi - - - neth,... the dark - ness is past, the
give thee light. The dark - ness is past,...... the

decres.
... the dark - ness is past, and the true light ...
the true light now shi - - - - - - - neth, .. the
dark - ness is past, the dark - - - - - - - - ness is past,
dark - ness is past, the dark - - - - - - - - - ness is past,
8va.
sf
decres.
V.
cres.
sempre.
now shi - - neth, the true light now shi - - - - - -
p
ff sempre.
dark - - ness is past. . . . . . . the true
the true light . . . . now shi - - neth, the
the true light, the true light now shi - -
loco.
ff
- - - - - - - - neth, now shi - - - - - - - neth. . . . .
. . . light now shi - - - - - - neth.
true light now shi - - - - - - - neth. . . . .
neth, the true light now shi - - - - - - - neth. . . . .
tutta forza.
Ped.
END OF PART FIRST.

SECOND PART.

THE ASCENSION.

No. 20. CHORUS.—THE SON OF MAN.

rit e dim.
pp
liv-er'd in-to the hands of sin-ful men, in-to the hands of sin - ful men;
liv-er'd in-to the hands of sin-ful men, in-to the hands of sin - ful men;
ritard e dim.
A
A tempo.
sf p
sf
he was cru - ci - fied, he was
he was cru - ci - fied, he was
(Brass.)
cru - ci-fied, he was cru - ci-fied, was cru - ci - fied,
he was cru - ci - fied, cru - ci - fied,
cru - ci-fied, he was cru - ci - fied, cru - ci - fied,
he was cru - - ci - fied,
f
riten.

B Allegro assai e giojoso. = 92.
and on the third day he rose .... a - gain, and
and on the third day he rose .... - a - gain, and
Allegro assai e giojoso.
f
(Trumpts.)
on the third day he rose .... a - gain,
on the third day he rose .... a - gain,
and on the third day he rose again,
and on the third day he rose a -
and on the third day he rose a -gain, he rose a - gain, the third......

and on the third day he rose a - gain,
and on the third day he rose a - gain, he rose a - gain,
gain, and on the
day he rose a - gain, and on the third day he rose a - gain, he
C
he was cru - ci - fied, he was cru - ci-fied, and
third day he rose a - gain, he was cru - ci - fied, he was cru - ci-fied, and
rose a - gain,
on the third day he rose a - gain, the third day he rose a - gain, the
on the third day he rose a - gain, the third day he rose a - gain, the
marcato.

third day, the third day, he rose a - gain, and
third day, the third day, he rose a - gain, and
sf
sf
sf
sf
sf
on the third day he rose .... a - gain, and on the third day he rose ....
on the third day he rose .... a - gain, and on the third day he rose ....
.... a - - gain.........................
.... a - - gain..........................

NO. 21. CHORAL.—JESUS, MY REDEEMER, LIVES.
♪= 72.
Soprano.
Alto.
Tenor.
Bass.
Accomp.
(Violins divided)
p dolce.
p
cres.
dim.
f
mp
sf
rit.
Je - sus, my Redeem - er, lives, Naught from him my soul can se - ver.
Bright the hope this prom - ise gives, I with him shall live for - ev - er.
Shall I fear then? can the head Rise and leave the members dead?

No. 22. Recit. and Solo.—AFTER THAT HE WAS RISEN.

sosten.
Peter. f
Si-mon, lov-est thou me? Yea Lord, thou knowest that I
dim e roll.
p
cres e agitato.
Tenor Solo.
love thee. Feed my sheep,
p
sf
feed my sheep.
sf p
dim e roll.
E sosten.
Peter.
Si-mon, lov-est thou me? lov-est thou me? Yea,
sf
Lord, thou know-est all things, thou

know - est, thou knowest that I love thee.
Tenor.
ad lib.
Feed my sheep, feed my sheep.
dolce.
ritard. pp
Arioso.—GO YE AND TEACH.
Maestoso. ♩ = 80.
Tenor Solo.
Accomp.
Go ye and teach all na - tions, bap - tizing them in the name of the
Fa - ther, and of the Son, and of the Ho - - ly Ghost;
dim.
Ped.
Ped.
teach - ing them to ob - serve all things, whatever I have command - ed

f
you. And lo! . . . . I am with you al - ways, I am
pp Ped.
ritard. molto.
with you al - ways, ev'n to the end, the end of the world.
Ped.
pp
No. 23. Recit.—AND HE LIFTED UP HIS HANDS.
Soprano Solo.
And he lift - ed up his hands and bless - ed them,
Accomp.
(Harp)
and it came to pass, while he blessed them, he was part-ed from them and
car - - ried up to heav'n.
p Ped.
Ped.
Ped.
Ped. ritard.
pp

No. 24. CHORUS.—IF YE THEN BE RISEN.

F
cres.
pp
Christ sit-teth on the right hand of God, if ye
Christ sit-teth on the right hand of God, if
f
pp
then be ris - en with Christ, seek those things which
if ye then be ris - en with Christ, seek those
ye.... then be ris - en with Christ, seek those things which
if - ye.... then be ris - en with
cres.
mf
are a - bove, seek those things,
things a - bove, seek those things........
are a - bove, if ye.... then be ri - - - -
Christ, if ye.... then be ris - en with Christ,

dim.
seek those things, seek those things which are a - bove,
seek those things which are a - bove,
ten. dim. cres.
sen, seek those things which are a - bove, seek
dim. pp cres.
seek those things which are a - bove, seek those....
dim. cres.
pp
f
G
p
which are a - bove, where Christ sit-teth on the
f p
which.... are a - bove,
f p
those things which are a - bove, where Christ sit-teth on the
f p
things which are a - bove,
p
f
cres. dimin.
right hand of God,............ pp where Christ sitteth on the right hand the right hand of
pp
cres. dimin.
right hand of God,............ pp where Christ sitteth on the right hand, the right hand of
pp
right hand of
ff pp
cres.
763958

H
dolce.
God,
if ye then be ris - en with
dolce.
God,
dim.
sf
p
Christ,
seek those things which are a - bove,......
seek those
are...... a - bove,
dolce.
if ye then be ri - sen with Christ,
seek those things,
dolce.
things, seek those things which are a - bove,
cres.
f
seek those things which are a - bove,
cres.
f
decres.
legato sempre.

I
p dolce.cres.poco a poco.
where Christ.... sit - teth on the
dolce.cres. poco a poco.
where Christ sit - teth on the
dolce. cres. poco a poco.
where Christ sit - teth on the
dolce. cres.. poco a poco.
on
dim.
pp
f
decres.
rall. e dim.
right hand of God, where Christ sit - teth on the right
rall e dim.
right hand of God, where Christ sit - teth on the right
rall. e dim.
the right hand,........................ the right
decres.
A tempo.
pp
hand of God....................
hand of God..................
a tempo
sf
pp
ppp

Recit.—AND PETER, WITH THE ELEVEN.
Contralto Solo.
And Peter, with the E-lev-en went forth to preach, the Lord working with .. ... them.
p
mf
p
No. 25.
Air.—O MAN OF GOD.
Allegro di molto.
=100.
Soprano Solo.
Accomp.
f animato.
O man of God, be strong in the Lord, and in the pow-er of his might,
O man of God, be strong . . . in the Lord, and in the pow-er of his might,
tr
f
marcato.
cres.
ff

J
Put on the whole......
ar - mor of God, and fight the good fight, the fight of
faith, and...... fight the good........ fight of
K
faith, lay hold
on e - ter - nal life...... where - un - to thou art call - ed,

lay hold on e - ter - nal life
where - un - to thou art call'd,
cres.
lay hold
on e - ter - nal life
ff sosten.
where - un - to
thou art call'd
ff
p cres.
tremolo.

f
p
cres.
L
f
O man of God, be
strong in the Lord, and in the pow-er of his might.
Put on the whole........
ar - mor of God, and fight the good'...'.... fight of

faith, the good fight,............... the fight of
sf p
sf p
sf p
faith,.............. lay hold on e-ter-nal life,
cres.
ff
ff
where-un-to thou............ art call'd, where-un-to
thou................................. art call------ed, thou art
ff
call'd..... .....
p cres.
ff
poco rit.

No. 26. Quartet.—FEED THE FLOCK OF GOD.

Adagio. ♪ = 96.

cantando. (*English horn.*)

accomp. sempre piano.

Vls Solo

tr tr

L.H. pp

poco rit. e dim.

Soprano Solo. *dolce.*

Feed the flock of God,

Alto Solo. *dolce.*

Feed the flock of God,

Tenor Solo.

Feed the

Bass Solo.

p

M
and when the chief shepherd shall appear,
and when the chief shep - herd shall ap - pear,
flock of God...... and when the chief shepherd shall ap - pear, thou
(Violin)
cres.
f
sf
cres.
dim.
thou wilt re-ceive a crown of glo - ry that fa - deth, fa-deth not a-way,
fa - deth not away,
wilt re-ceive a crown of glo - ry that fa - deth not a - way,
dolce.
Feed the
sf
p
feed the flock of God,
feed the flock of God........ the flock of God,
feed the flock
flock of God,.... the flock of God,

and when the chief .... shep - herd shall .... ap -
and when the chief .... shepherd shall .... ap -
of God, ... and when - the chief shepherd shall ap -
and when the chief shep - herd shall .... ap -
tr
L.H.
N
poco piu mosso e animato.
mf
f
a tempo
dolce.
pear, thou wilt receive a crown of glo - ry, thou wilt receive a crown of glo - ry that
pear, thou wilt receive a crown of glo - ry, thou wilt receive a crown of glo - ry,
poco piu mosso.
a tempo.
fa - deth not a - way, ... fa - deth not a - way, ...
that fa - deth not a - way, fa - deth not away,

sf
legato.
0
feed the
feed the flock of God,
feed the flock of God,
p
poco rit.
a tempo
flock of God.... and when the chief shepherd shall appear thou wilt receive a crown of
the flock of God,....
and when the chief shep - herd shall appear thou wilt receive a crown of
and when the chief shepherd shall appear,
p
cres.

cres.
glo - ry, a crown of glo - ry that fa - - - deth not, thou wilt receive a crown of
a crown of glo - - ry that fa - deth
glo - ry, a crown of glo - ry, that fa - deth
f
dim.
p
rit.
pp
glo - ry, a crown of glo - ry that fa - deth not, fa - deth not a - way.
not,
not, a crown of glo - ry that fadeth not, fa - deth not a - way.
(Violin Solo.)
a tempo.
Dim.
(Engl. Horn.)
ritard poco.
ppp

PENTECOST.

No. 27. Recit.—AND WHEN THE DAY OF PENTECOST WAS COME.

Tenor Solo.

Accomp.

Allegro maestoso e con fuoco. ♩ = 108.

ad lib.

And when the day of Pentecost was come,

f dim. p f

ad lib.

the a-pos-tles were all to-geth-er in one place,

a tempo. f a tempo. p ppp

And sud-den-ly there came a sound from heav'n

poco a poco cres. mf

cres. ff

as of a migh-ty rush-ing wind,

8 ff sempre. cres.

and it fill-ed all the house where they were

8va

N
sit - - - - - ting; and
Ped.
ff
*
pp
cres. poco a poco.
cres.
there ap-pear-ed un-to them clo-ven tongues as of
ff
fire; and it sat up-on each of them.
mf dim e ritard.
a tempo.
ff
pp
p
And they were all fill-ed with the Ho - - - - ly Ghost,
p dim.
pp
p dim.
pp
a tempo.
rit.
rall.
and began to speak in oth-er tongues, as the spir-it gave them ut-ter-ance.
sf
sf
sf
sf
p

No. 28.
Chorus.—THE VOICE OF THE LORD.
Allegro con fuoco. ♩= 152.
Soprano.
Alto.
Tenor.
Bass.
Accomp.
The voice of the Lord di - vid - eth the
The voice of the Lord di - vid - eth the
Allegro con fuoco.
flames of fire, the voice of the Lord di - vid - eth the
the voice.......... of the Lord di -
flames of fire, the voice of the Lord di - vid - eth the
flames of fire, the Lord di-vid - eth the flames of fire.
vid - eth the flames,
flames of fire, di-vid - eth the flames of fire.
the voice of the Lord,

The voice of the Lord is full of ma - jes - ty,
and
The voice of the Lord is full of ma - jes - ty, and
ff
and ev - e - ry one doth speak of his
ev - e - ry one,
and ev' - ry one doth speak of his
cres.
glo - - - - ry
dim.

P
the voice of the
the voice of the
Lord di - vid - eth the flames of fire.........
The voice............
Lord di - vid - eth the flames of fire.........
The voice........
The voice
of the Lord is full
of......
of the
of the Lord is full,............ is full
of......
The voice
of the Lord,

ma - jes - ty, his voice is full of ma - - - - - jes - ty,
ma - jes - ty, his voice is full of ma - - - - - jes - ty,
Q
and ev - e - ry one, doth speak of his
doth speak
and ev' - ry one doth speak of his
and ev - e - ry one doth speak of his

glo - - - - - - - ry, doth speak of his glo - -
of his glo - - - - ry, of his
glo - - ry, and ev' - ry one doth speak of his
glo - - - - - - - - - - - - ry, and ev' - ry,
- - - - ry and ev'-ry one doth speak of his
glo - - ry,
glo - - - ry and ev'-ry one doth speak of his
one doth speak of his glo - - - - - - - - -
glo - - - - - - ry.
glo - - - - - - ry.
- - - - - - - - ry.
dim.
cres.
decres.

dim.
R
The voice of the Lord di - vid - eth the
The voice of the Lord di. - vid - eth the

flames of fire, the voice of the Lord di - vid - eth the
the voice.......... of the Lord di -
flames of fire, the voice of the Lord di - vid - eth the
flames of fire, the Lord di-vid - eth the flames of fire.
vid - eth the flames,
flames of fire, di-vid - eth the flames of fire.
the voice of the Lord,
cres.
f
The voice of the Lord is full of ma - jes - ty,
The voice of the Lord is full of ma - jes - ty, and
mp

doth speak of his glo - - ry,
ev - e - ry one doth speak of his glo - - ry,
one doth speak of his glo - - ry,
T
cres.
the voice of the Lord is
cres.
the voice of the Lord
cres.
the voice of the Lord is
pp
cres.
the voice of the Lord is full
pp
cres. poco a poco.
f
cres.
ff
full of ma - - - - jes - ty, and ev' - ry
full of ma - - - - jes - ty, and ev' - ry
f
cres.
ff
ff sempre.

ff sempre.
one doth speak........ of his glo - - - - - - - - -
ff sempre.
one doth speak........ of his glo - - - - - - - - -
ry, ev' - - - - - ry one doth speak of his glo - -
ry, ev' - - - - - ry one doth speak of his glo - -
ritard. a tempo.
- - - - - - - - - - - - - ry.........................
ritard. a tempo.
- - - - - - - - - - - - - ry.........................
ff
ritard. a tempo.

RECIT.—NOW WHEN THIS WAS NOISED ABROAD.

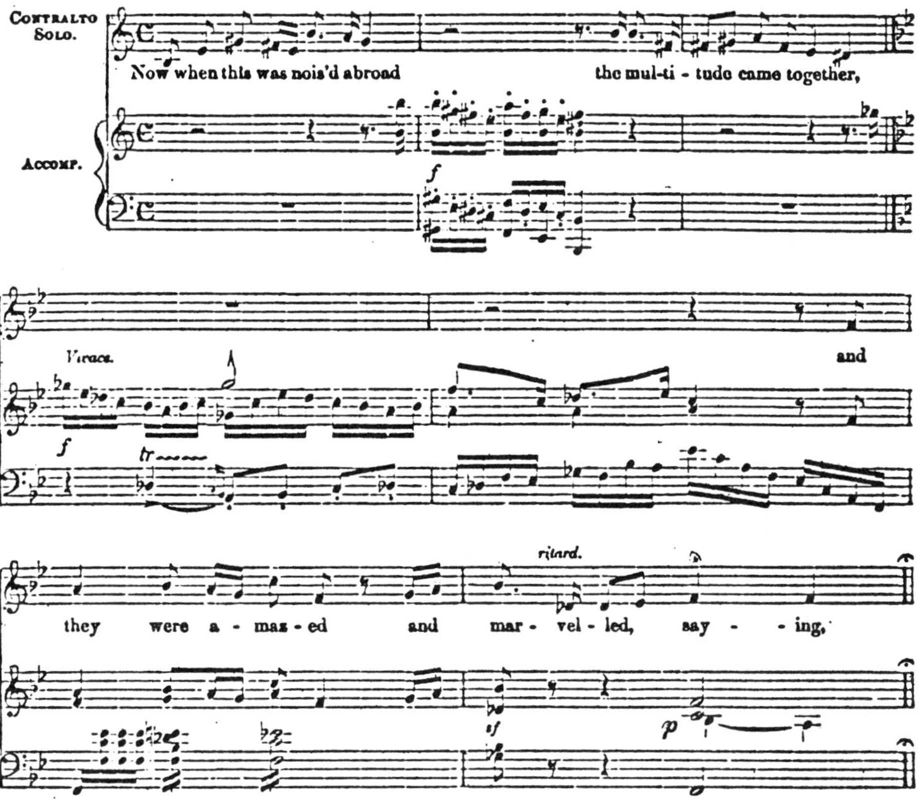

CONTRALTO SOLO.

Now when this was nois'd abroad the mul-ti - tude came together,

ACCOMP.

f

Vivace.

f *tr*

and they were a - maz-ed and mar - vel - led, say - - ing,

ritard.

sf *p*

le - ans? be- hold, are not all these who speak Gal - i - le - ans?
le - ans? be- hold, are not all these who speak Gal - i - le - ans?
be-hold, are not, are not all these who speak Gal - i - le - ans?
and how is it that we ev' - ry one hear them in our own tongue,
and how is it that we ev' - ry one, and how is it that we ev' - ry one, hear them in our own
where - in we were born? and how is it that we hear them
tongue, where - in we were born? and how is it that we hear them
be - hold,

speaking in our tongues the won - derful works of God? behold, are not
speak - ing in our tongues
speaking in our tongues the won - derful works of God? and how is it that we
not................ all these who speak Gali - le - ans?
ff
all.... these who speak Gal - i - le - ans? and how is it that we
ev' - ry one hear them in our own tongue, and how, how
and how is it, how is it that
ritard.
hear them speak-ing in our tongues the won - der - ful works of God?
that we hear them speaking of the won - - derful works of God?
is it that we hear them speaking of the won - der - ful works of God?
we hear them speaking in our tongues the won - der - ful works of God?

RECITATIVE.—BUT PETER STANDING UP.

And it shall come to pass in the
last days, saith God, that I will pour out my spir - it up-
- on all flesh; and your sons and daughters shall
prophesy, and your young men shall see vis - ions,
mf
mp.
ff
p dolce.

rit.
dim.
dim.
and your old men shall dream dreams, your old men shall
ten.
sf
pp
ten.
rit.
pp
V
dream . . . . dreams.
poco piu mosso. ♩= 126.
rit.
ppp
pp
cres.
f sempre.
And I will show wonders in heav'n a-
f
-bove, and signs on the earth be-neath,
pp cres.
f
ff
blood and fire, and va-por of
cres.
ff

W
p
smoke;
pp
sf p
cres.
the sun shall be turned in-to dark-ness,
p il basso marcato.
cres.
sf
p
sf
and the moon shall be turn-ed in-to blood,
f
be-fore the day of the
cres.
sf
sf
sf
ff
poco rit.
X
Lord.... com-eth, the great and no-ta-ble day,
a tempo.
fz
fz
ff
ff marcato.
the sun shall be turned in-to
p

sf
cres.
dark-ness, the moon shall be turned in - to blood, be - fore the day of the Lord
ritard.
Y.
com - - - - - - - - - - - eth, the great and no-ta-ble day,
a tempo.
f
p
mf
f
and I will pour out my spir - it up-on all flesh, saith God, and
p
I will pour out my spir - it up - on all flesh, and
dolce.

ev - ery one that call - eth on the name of the - Lord shall be
saved, and I will pour out my spir - it up - -
on all flesh,
Z.
and ev - ery one that call - eth, that
call - - eth on the Lord, and ev - ery one that call - eth on the
name of the Lord, that call - eth on the Lord, shall be sa - ved, be
f
p

sav - - - ed.
mf
dim.
ritard.
p
dim.
pp
No. 31.
Air—AS FOR MAN.
Larghetto. ♩ = 69.
espressivo.
Contralto Solo.
Accomp.
pp
As for man his days are as
grass, as.... a flow - er of the field he flour - ish - eth,
riten.
dolce.
as for man his days are as grass, as a flow - er of the
dolce.

field, as a flow - er he flour - - ish-eth, as a flower of the
dolce.
A più mosso. ♩ = 92.
field he flour - - ish-eth, For the
pp
sempre legato.
wind.................... pass - eth o - ver it,
cres. poco a poco.
sf ff
riten.
and it is gone; and the place there -
a tempo.
ppp
ppp
pp
riten.
of shall know it no more, shall
sf ff

B
know it no more,
Tempo primo.
as for man his days.... are as grass;
riten poco.
piu mosso.
as...... a flow - er of the field, he flourisheth. For the
wind pass-eth o - - - - ver it, and it is
gone; and the place.... there of shall know it no
cres.

more........ shall know it no more. But the word of the
Lord en - dur - eth for - ev - er, but the word of the Lord en -
dur - eth for - ev - er, and this is the word, the word which is preached to you,
and his word en - dur - eth for-ev - - - er.
riten. poco.
a tempo.
rit.
dim.
pp
ppp
p
f

No. 32. Recitative.—YE MEN OF ISRAEL.

RECIT.—NOW WHEN THEY HEARD THIS.

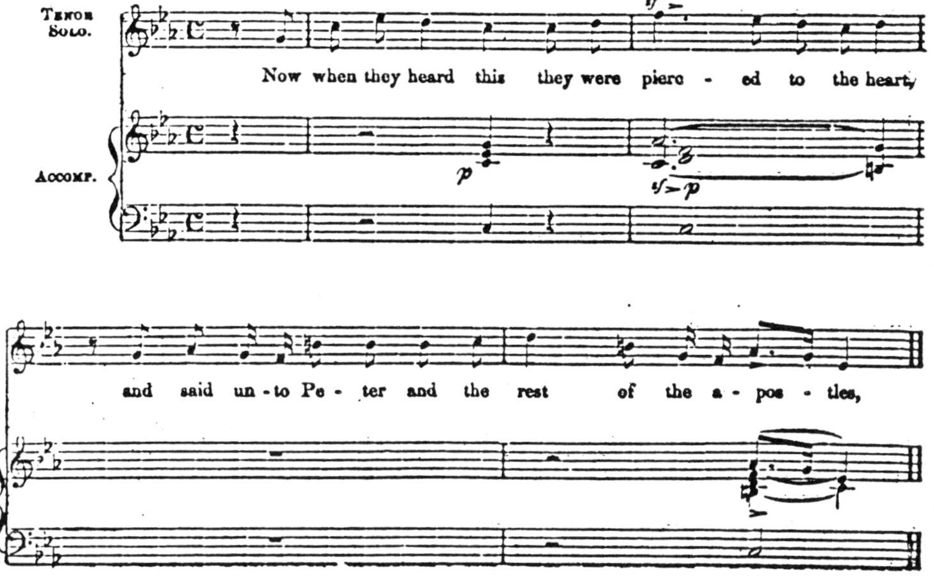

No. 33. CHORUS.—MEN AND BRETHREN.

decres.
dim.
shall we do? what shall we do to be sav - ed?
decres.
dim.
decres.
dim.
.... ved? what shall.... we do to be- sav - ed?
dim.
p
decres.
what shall we do to be sav - ed?
decres.
p
ff
men and breth - ren, what shall we do to be sav -
ff
ff
men and breth - ren, what shall we do to be sav'd....
ff
f
sosten.
- - - - - - - - - - ed?..........................
.... to be.... sav - - - ed?...........................
.... be sav - - ed?..........................
.... to be.... sav - - - ed?..........................
ff sempre.
Ped.
Ped.

No. 34. Recit. and Solo.—REPENT, AND BE BAPTISED.

Bass Solo. Peter.

Accomp. Grave. ♩ = 50. (Trombones.) *f* *p* *mf* *p*

Re - pent, re-pent, and be bap - tis - ed, ev' - ry one of you,

In the name of Je-sus Christ, for the forgiveness of sins, and ye shall receive the gift of the

p *sf*

Ho - ly Ghost.

Andante. 𝅗𝅥 = 66. cres. *sf* *p* dolce cres. *f*

Andante con moto. 𝅗𝅥 = 88.

sf *p*

For the prom - ise is to you and your chil - - dren, and to

all that are a - far off, as many as the Lord our God shall

ritard.

C The Twelve Disciples.
1st. Tenors.
2nd. Tenors.
1st. Basses.
2nd. Basses.
Accomp.
For the prom-ise is to you and your chil - dren, and to
Solo.
For the prom-ise is to you and your chil - - dren, and to
call,
a tempo.
all that are a-far off, as many as the Lord our God shall call, the
riten.
a tempo.
all, all that are a-far off, as many as the Lord our God shall call, as
prom-ise is to you and all that are a-far off, as many as the Lord our
man - y as the Lord our God, as many as the Lord our
Lord............ as many as the

Recitative.—WHILE PETER YET SPAKE.

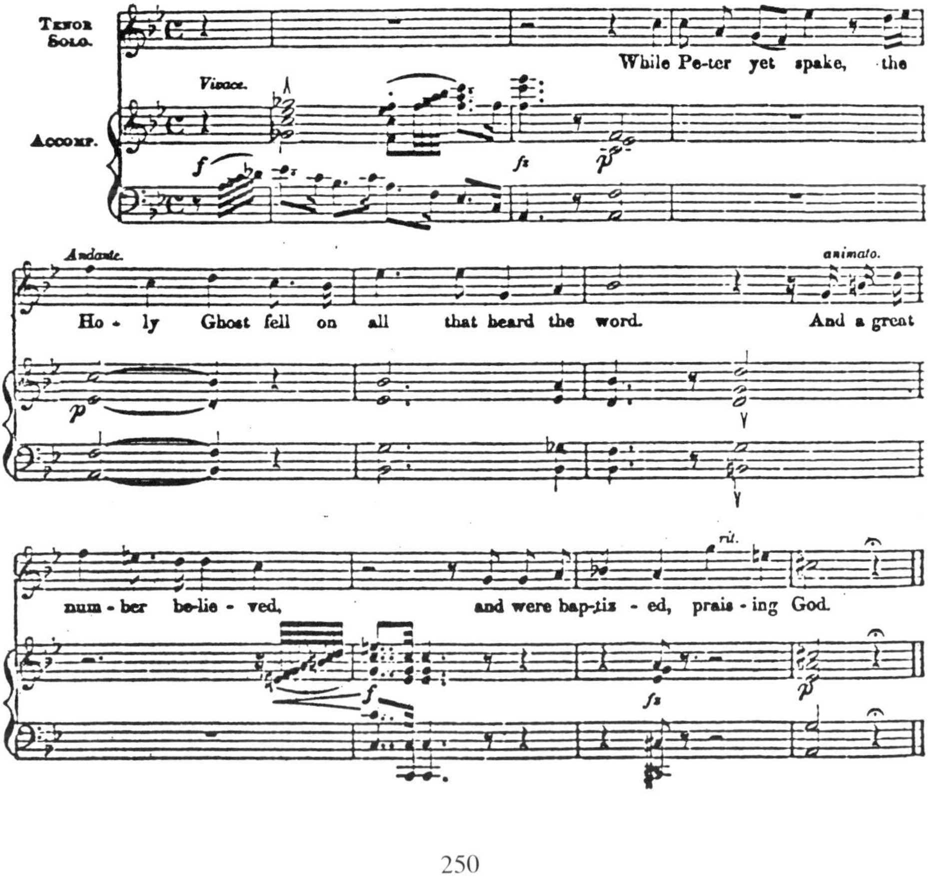

Tenor Solo.

Accomp.

Vivace. *f* *fz* *p*

While Pe-ter yet spake, the

Andante. *p*

Ho - ly Ghost fell on all that heard the word.

animato.

And a great num - ber be-lie - ved,

f *fz* *rit.* *p*

and were bap-tiz - ed, prais - ing God.

No. 35. Chorus.—THIS IS THE WITNESS OF GOD.
Allegro Moderato. ♩ = 92.
Soprano.
Alto.
Tenor.
Bass.
Accomp.
Cantando.
mf
Dim.
This is the witness of God.... which he hath tes-ti-fied of his Son, which he hath tes-ti - fied...... of his
This is the witness of God,...... which he hath tes-ti - fied of his
Son, This is the witness of God, which he hath
Son he hath tes - - -
This is the witness of God,.....................................
This is the witness of God, which he hath
f
sf
8va

tes - ti - fied........ .... of his Son,
this is the witness of
ti - fied of.......... his Son.
this is the witness of God.
tes - ti - fied of his Son.
God.
D
We know that the Son of
sf Dim.
Cres.
God is come,
and hath giv'n us un - der -
We know that the Son of God is come, and hath giv'n us un - der -

standing, that we may know the True One, hath
standing, that we may know the True One, and hath giv'n us under-
p Dolce.
giv'n us under-standing, that we may know the
standing, that we may know the True One, the
Cres.
True One, we know that the Son of God is come, and hath
E
True One, the True One, and hath

f Dim. f Dim. p
giv - - - en us under-stand - - - - - ing, that
f dim
giv'n us un - der - stand - ing, that we may know,
f Dim. f Dim. p
giv'n...... us under - stand - - - - ing, that
Dim. f Dim.
giv'n us un - der - stand - ing, that we may know,
f Dim. f Dim. p
Dim. ten. pp Sempre.
we may know the True
p dim. ten. pp Sempre.
that we may know, the True
Dim. ten. pp Sempre.
we p may know dim. pp the True
that we may know the True
Dim.
pp
F
pp Sempre.
One, The True One,
pp Sempre.
One, The True One,
pp
Cres. poco a poco.

f
This is the witness of God, which he hath
This is the witness of God, which he hath
f
tes-ti-fied of his Son,
which he hath tes - ti -
This is the wit-ness of God....... which he hath
tes-ti-fied of his Son,
Dim.
f
Dim.
tied of his Son,
f
This is the wit-ness of
tes-ti-fied of his Son,
This is the witness of God,
God,....................
Dim.
f
f

G
God, which he.......... hath tes-ti-fied
God, which he hath tes--ti--fied
this is the wit-ness of
... . which he hath tes-ti--fied of his
this is the wit-ness of God, which he hath
sosten.
this is the wit---ness of
God,
Son, this...... is the wit----ness,
Dim.
tes----ti--fied,... .... hath tes-ti-fied....... of his
God, which he hath tes-ti-fied....... of his
the wit-ness of God, which he hath tes-ti-fied....... of his
he hath tes-ti--fied.... .... of his
Dim.

H
pp
mf
Son.
We know that the Son of God is
pp mf sosten.
Son. We know that the Son of God is come, We know that the Son of God is
pp
mf
Son.
We know that the Son of God
Legato sempre.
pp
Cres. poco a poco
f
Cres.
come, and hath giv'n us understanding that we may know the True One, that
come, and hath giv'n us under-stand-ing that we may know the True One, that
f
Cres.
come, and hath giv-en us under-standing that we may know the True One,
come, and hath giv-en us under-stand-ing that we may know the
f
Cres.
ff
Dim.
ff we may know, may know Dim. the True One.
ff we may know............... Dim. the True One.
This is the wit-ness of God...... which he hath testi-fied of his Son.
ff
Dim.
True One, that we may know, may know the True One.
ff
Dim.
p

No. 36. CHORAL.—PRAISE TO THE FATHER.

ff
O my soul, wake!........
mf
Harp, lute and
psal - ter - y take,
f
Sound forth thy glad ad - o - ra - -
tion..............
decres.
Ped.
Wind inst.
Harps
dim.
p
cres.
tr
Ped. poco rit. e dim.
p

Recitative.—AND PETER SAID.

Soprano Solo.
Peter.
And Pe - ter said, Go and tell these things to the breth - ren.
Accomp.
p
p

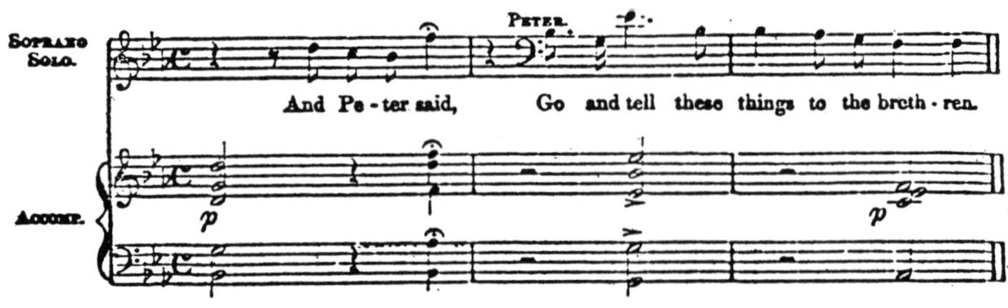

No. 37. Solo and Chorus.—NOW AS YE WERE REDEEMED.

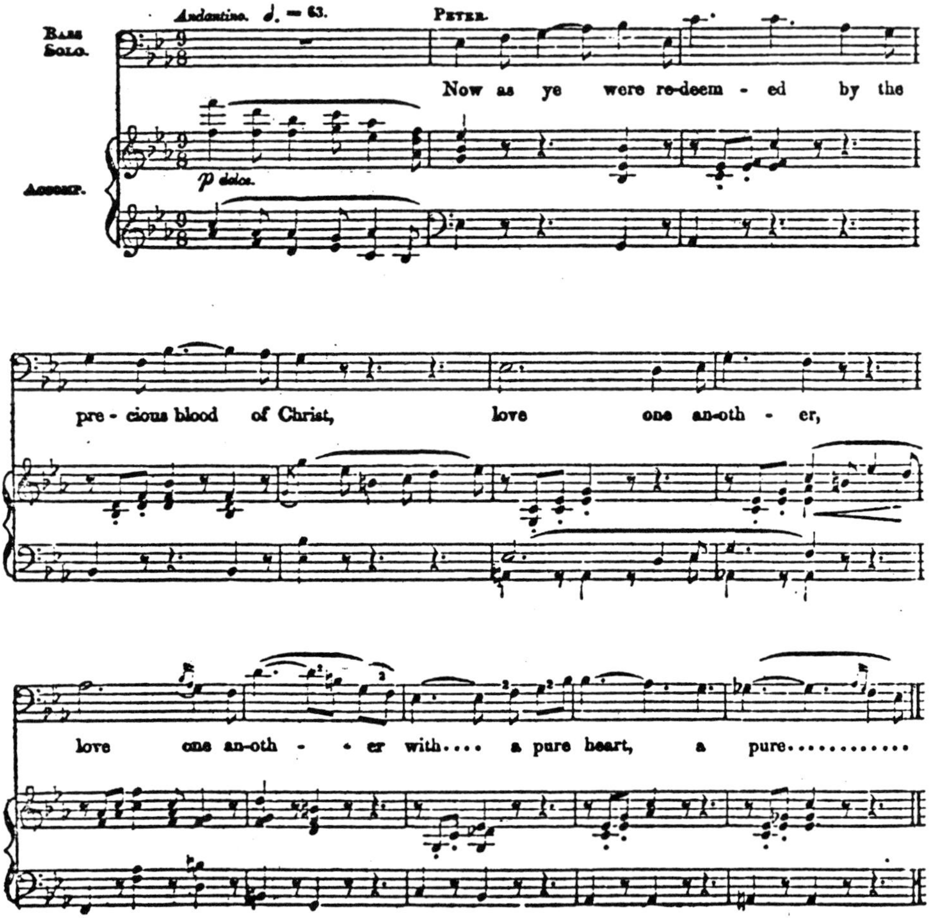
Andantino. ♩. = 63.
Bass Solo.
Peter.
Now as ye were re-deem - ed by the
Accomp.
p dolce.
pre - cious blood of Christ, love one an-oth - er,
love one an-oth - - er with.... a pure heart, a pure............

PETER.
BASS SOLO.
heart.
THE DISCIPLES.
TENORS.
BASSES.
SOPRANO.
ALTO.
TENOR.
BASS.
ACCOMP.
CHORUS.
pp
Be-lov - ed, let us love.... one anoth - er,
Be-lov - ed, let us love.... one anoth - er,
for love is of God,
and may the tri-al
cres.
f
p

of your faith be found un-to praise, honor and glo-ry,
cres.
let us love one an-oth er,
cres.
p
be-lov-ed,
p
let us love one an-oth-er,
for
p
p
p
be-lov-ed,
p
sf
p
cres.
mf
sosten.
re - ceiv - - - - - - ing the sal-
for love is of God,
love is of God,
p
for love.......... is of God,
p
p
for love is of God, is of God,
for love is...... of God,

rit. poco
va - tion of your.... souls.
p
a tempo.
sf
p CHORUS.
Now as we were redeem - ed by the precious blood of
p CHORUS.
p CHORUS.
Now as we were redeem - ed by the precious blood of
p CHORUS.
poco rit.
p
PETER.
and
Christ, let us love one an - oth - er, one an - oth -
dim.
let us love one an - oth -
dim.
Christ, let us love one an - oth - - er, one an - oth -
dim.
Christ, let us love one an - oth - er, one an - oth -
dim.

K
may the tri - al of your faith be found unto praise, hon - or and glo - ry,
er; for love is of God, for love is of
er; for love is of God,
and may the . tri - al of your faith be .... found un - to
and may the tri - al of your faith,
God,........ is of God, let us love one an -
one

praise, hon - or and glo - ry, re - ceiv - - - - ing
be found un - to praise, hon - or and glo - ry, re - ceiv - - ing
cres.
oth - - er, for love is of God, let us love one an -
an-oth - er for............................ love............
be-lov - ed, let us love one an - oth - er, let us love one an -
for love....... is of God, love...........
riten.
the sal-va - tion of your.... souls, re - ceiv - ing the sal-vation of your
dim.
the sal-va - tion of your...... souls,
your.... souls,
oth -er, for love is of God,..............
is of God,.... love is of God,
oth -er, for love is of God,.............
.. is of God,.................

ritard. a tempo.

souls, ... of your souls.

pp a tempo.

of your souls.

pp a tempo.

ritard. pp sempre. a tempo.

love is of God.

ritard. pp sempre. a tempo.

ritard. pp sempre. a tempo.

love is of God.

ritard. pp sempre. a tempo.

ritard. a tempo. rit.

pp sempre. pp dim.

Recitative.—AND THEN THEY GLORIFIED GOD.

No. 38. **Duet.—SING UNTO GOD.**

O sing........... un - to God,
who call'd us out of dark - ness,
who call'd us out of dark - ness,
in -
to his won - - - derful light, ...
in - to his won - - - derful light, ...
in - to..............
in - to..............
dim.
cres. poco a poco.
f cres.
Ped.

sf > rit.
. . . . his won-der - ful light,
sf > rit.
. . . . . his won-der - ful light,
a tempo.
tr
p
M
Sing un-to God, sing praises to his
tr
dolce.
ho - ly name, sing un - to God, sing prais-es to his ho - ly name,
sing un - to God, sing praises to his name,
sing un - to God, sing praises to his ho - ly name,
p sempre.
sf > mf

O sing .... un - to
O sing .... un - to
8va
cres.
f marcato.
God, who call'd us out of dark - ness in - to his wonderful
God, who call'd us out of dark - ness in - to his wonderful
p
dolce.
N
light, who call - - - - - - - - - - ed
light, who call - - - - - - - - - - ed
pp
cres.
fz cres.
ff
Ped.
us out of dark - ness in - to his won - derful light, in - to his
us out of dark - ness in - to his wonder - ful......

wonderful light, his won - - - - - - - - - der - ful
light, his won - - - - - - - - - der - ful
pp cres. poco a poco.
light, sing
light, sing un - to God,
sf
sf
un - to God,
O
O
cres.
f marcato.
sing . . . . . un - to God, sing prais - - - - - es
f
sing . . . . . un - to God, sing prais - - - - - es
decres.

to his ho - - ly name, his ho - - ly name,
to his ho - ly, his ho - ly name, sing un - to God, who
out of dark - ness in - to his
call'd us out of dark - ness, out of dark - - - ness in - to
f sosten.
won - - - - - - der - ful light.
f sosten.
his won - der - ful light.
ff sempre.
Ped.

No. 39.
Chorus.—GREAT AND MARVELLOUS.
Allegro moderato e maestoso.
Soprano.
Alto.
Tenor.
Bass.
Allegro moderato e maestoso.
Marcato.
♩ = 88.
♩ = 108.
mp cres.
Trumpets
Accomp.
Great............... and mar- - - vel-lous,
Great................ and mar- - - vel-lous,
mar - - - - - - vel- lous,
great and marvellous are thy works, Lord God Al-
great and marvellous are thy works, are thy works, Lord God Al-

P
ff
might - - - - - y;
f sosten.
just and true are thy
ways, thou King of saints. All na-tions shall come and wor -
ship be - fore thee, for thy judg - ments are made
All nations shall come and worship
be - fore are....................
just and true are thy ways, thou King of saints. All nations shall come and
wor - ship be - fore thee, for thy judg - ments are made
All na - tions shall
wor - - ship thee,

Piu Allegro. 𝅗𝅥 = 132.
man - - i - fest. We praise thee, O Lord, and glo - ri - fy thy
.... made man - i - fest.
man - - i - fest. We praise thee, O Lord, and glo - ri - fy thy
Piu Allegro.
A capella. 𝅗𝅥 = 84.
not too fast.
rit.
name for e - ver - more. A - - men,
name for e - ver - more, A - men, we
mf
we praise thee, O Lord, we
A capella.
we praise thee, O Lord, and glo - ri - fy thy name,
we
praise thee, O Lord, and glo - ri - fy thy name,
praise thee and glo - ri - fy.............. thy name,

f cres.
thy name for e - vermore, and glo - ri - fy thy name for
cres.
praise thee, O Lord,
f cres.
and glo - ri - fy thy name for
we praise thee, O Lord, and
f cres.
ff sempre.
e - ver - more, A - men, we
ff sempre.
e - ver - more, A - men, we
ff sempre.
mf
ff
praise thee, O Lord, and glo - ri - fy thy name, we praise thee, O
praise thee, O Lord,
we praise thee, we praise thee, O
praise thee, O Lord, we praise thee, we praise

Lord, and glo - ri - fy thy name for e - - - - ver-more, we
Lord, and glo - ri - fy thy name for e - - - - ver-more, we
thee, O Lord, and glo - ri - fy thy name for e - ver-more,
ff decres.
p
poco rit.
dim.
praise thee for e - ver - more, A - - - -
ff decres.
praise thee for e - ver - more, A - - -
thy name for e - ver more, A - - - - -
ff decres.
p dim
pp
ppp a tempo.
S
p
men, we
ppp a tempo.
pp
men, we praise thee, O Lord, we
men, we praise thee; O Lord, and glo - ri - fy thy name
ppp
pp

cres. poco a poco.
cres. e accel. poco a poco.
praise thee, O Lord, and glo - ri - fy thy name for e - ver-more, and glo - ri -
cres. poco a poco.
cres. e accel. poco a poco.
praise thee, O Lord, and glo - ri - fy thy name for e - ver-more, and
mf
we praise thee, O Lord
mf
cres. poco a poco.
cres e accel. poco a poco.
fy thy name for e - ver-more, A - - - - men, A - -
for e - ver-more, A -
glo - ri - fy thy name,
and glo - ri - fy thy
men, for e - ver - more, A - - - - men,
men, A - - - - - men,
for e - ver - more, A - - men. A - -
name for e - ver - more A - -

Più Allegro. ff
great and mar - - vel - lous
ff
ff
- - - men, great and mar - - vel - lous
ff
Più allegro. 𝅗𝅥 = 100.
ff
are............ thy works,............ Lord
are............ thy works,............ Lord
fff sosten.
God Al - might - - - - y;..............
fff sosten.
God Al - might - - - - y;..............
fff Ped.

T Molto allegro. 𝅗𝅥 = 112.
pp
cres.
All na - - tions shall come.... and wor - ship.... be -
All na - tions, all na - tions shall come
Molto allegro.
f
fore.............. thee, for thy judg - - ments, thy judg - - ments
shall come and wor - - - - ship be - fore.... thee,
and wor - - ship be - fore...... thee......
and wor - ship be - fore thee, for thy....
are made man - i - fest, are made man - i -
for.... thy judg - ments
.. for thy judg - - ments are made man - i -
judg - - ments, thy judg - ments are............. made man - i -

ff
fest. We praise............ thee, O Lord,
ff
fest. We praise............. thee, O Lord,
ff
and glo - ri - fy thy
ff
U
p
cres.
O Lord, we praise........ thee, and
p
we praise.................... thee,
p
cres.
O Lord, we praise........ thee, and
name for e - ver - more, we praise................. thee,
p
f
dim.
glo - - - ri - fy.................... thy name for e -
f
dim.
.. and glo - ri - fy........ thy name for e -
f
dim.
glo - - ri - fy..................... thy name for e -
f
dim.
and glo - - fy thy name................. for
f sosten.
dim.

p cres. f
- ver - more, A - men, A - men, for
- ver - - more,
p cres. f
- ver - more, for e - - - - ver - more, ... A -
p cres. f
e - ver - more, A - men, for e - ver - more,
p cres. f
ff poco rit. a tempo.
e - ver - more, A - - men.
e - - - ver - more,
ff poco rit. a tempo.
men, A - men, A - - men,
ff poco. rit. a tempo. p
p cres. f al fine. poco rit.
A - - - - - - men, ... A - - men. . . .
A - - - - - - - men, A - - - men. . . .
p cres. f al fine. poco rit.
A - - - - - - men, A - - - - - men. . . . .
A - - - - - - men, A - - - - - men. . . .
cres. f al fine poco ritard.
A. B. KIDDER'S MUSIC TYPOGRAPHY.
THE END.

1776—1876.

BY APPOINTMENT OF THE U. S. CENTENNIAL COMMISSION.

THE CENTENNIAL MEDITATION OF COLUMBIA.

A CANTATA

FOR

THE INAUGURAL CEREMONIES

AT

PHILADELPHIA, MAY 10, 1876.

POEM BY

SIDNEY LANIER,

OF GEORGIA.

MUSIC BY

DUDLEY BUCK,

OF CONNECTICUT.

NEW YORK:

G. SCHIRMER, 701 BROADWAY.

THE CENTENNIAL MEDITATION OF COLUMBIA.

From this hundred-terraced height
Sight more large with nobler light
Ranges down yon towering years:
Humbler smiles and lordlier tears
  Shine and fall, shine and fall,
While old voices rise and call
Yonder where the to-and-fro
Weltering of my Long-Ago
Moves about the moveless base
Far below my resting-place.

Mayflower, Mayflower, slowly hither flying,
Trembling Westward o'er yon balking sea,
Hearts within *Farewell dear England* sighing,
Winds without *But dear in vain* replying,
Gray-lipp'd waves about thee shouted, crying
    No! It shall not be!

Jamestown, out of thee—
Plymouth, thee—thee, Albany—
Winter cries, *Ye freeze: away!*
Fever cries, *Ye burn: away!*
Hunger cries, *Ye starve: away!*
Vengeance cries, *Your graves shall stay!*

Then old Shapes and Masks of Things,
Framed like Faiths or clothed like Kings—
Ghosts of Goods once fleshed and fair,
Grown foul Bads in alien air—
War, and his most noisy lords,
Tongued with lithe and poisoned swords—

Error, Terror, Rage and Crime,
All in a windy night of time
Cried to me from land and sea,
No! Thou shalt not be!

Hark!
Huguenots whispering *yea* in the dark,
Puritans answering *yea* in the dark!
Yea, like an arrow shot true to his mark,
Darts through the tyrannous heart of Denial.
Patience and Labor and solemn-souled Trial,
Foiled, still beginning,
Soiled, but not sinning,
Toil through the stertorous death of the Night,
Toil, when wild brother-wars new-dark the Light,
Toil, and forgive, and kiss o'er, and replight.

Now Praise to God's oft-granted grace,
Now Praise to Man's undaunted face,
Despite the land, despite the sea,
I was: I am: and I shall be—
How long, Good Angel, O how long?
Sing me from Heaven a man's own song!

"Long as thine Art shall love true love,
Long as thy Science truth shall know,
Long as thine Eagle harms no Dove,
Long as thy Law by law shall grow,
Long as thy God is God above,
Thy brother every man below,
So long, dear Land of all my love,
Thy name shall shine, thy fame shall glow!"

O Music, from this height of time my Word unfold:
In thy large signals all men's hearts Man's Heart behold:
Mid-heaven unroll thy chords as friendly flags unfurled,
And wave the world's best lover's welcome to the world.

SIDNEY LANIER.

CENTENNIAL CANTATA.

Poem by SYDNEY LANIER.*

Music by DUDLEY BUCK.*

* By appointment of the U. S. Centennial Commission.

Soprano.
cres.
p From this hun - dred - ter - raced height, Sight more large with
Alto.
Tenor.
cres.
p From this hun - dred - ter - raced height, Sight more large........
Bass.
Sight more large with
Str. pizz.
arco.
p
cres.
no - bler light Ran - ges down yon tow'r - - ing
no - - bler light
f
.... with no - bler light Ran - ges down yon tow'r - ing
no - bler light
Tr.
f

p
years:
Hum - - bler smiles - and lord - - - lier
p
years:
Hum - - bler smiles and lord - - lier
dim.
p
Vcelli. Eng. Horn.
p
tears
Shine and fall,
Shine and fall,
p
tears, Shine and fall, ... Shine and fall, ... While old voi - ces
Shine and fall,
Shine and fall,

crescendo poco a poco.
f
While old voi - ces rise and call, Yon - der where the to - and-fro
crescendo poco a poco.
f
rise and call, Yon - der where the to - and-fro
While old voi - ces rise and call,
crescendo poco à poco.
f
p
Wel - t'ring of my Long - A - go, Moves a - bout the move - less
p
Wel - t'ring of my Long - A - go, Moves a - bout the move - less
p
pizz.

base,
Far...... be - low my rest - - ing place.
Far................ be - low my rest - - ing place.
ase,
Far...... be - low my rest - - ing place.
arco. p
pp
Fl.
Ob.
Clar.
Cor.
p
Fag.
Vc.
p

B
un poco agitato.
mf
p
mf Semi-Chorus.
May - - flower,
May - - flower,
Semi-Chorus.
mf
May - - flower,

p
slow - ly hith - er fly - ing,
p
Semi-Chorus.
mf
Trem - - bling
p
mf
West - - - ward o'er yon balk - ing sea,
Semi-Chorus.
mf
p

p
mf
Hearts with - in "Fare - well, ... Fare - well, dear
p
mf
Hearts with - in "Fare - well, ... Fare - well, dear
tr
5-1
p
p
dim.
Eng - land," sigh - - - - - - - - - - - - - ing,
dim.
Eng - land," sigh - - - - - - - - - - - - - ing,

Full Chorus.
pp
Winds with-out "But dear in vain" re - - ply - - - -
Full Chorus.
pp
Winds with-out "But dear in vain" re - - ply - - -
p
p
mf
cres.
ing, Gray - - lipp'd waves a - bout thee shout - ed,
mf
cres.
ing, Gray - - lipp'd waves a - bout thee shout - ed,
cres.
sempre cres.

sf
cry - - - - - - - - ing,
ff "No! . . . .
sf
cry - - - - - - - - ing,
ff "No! . . . .
sf
ff
sff
Ped.
sf
No! . . . .
It shall not be!"
sf
No! . . . .
It shall not be!"
sff
sf
fp
Ped.

Semi-Chorus. mf
James - - town,
C
Semi-Chorus. mf
p
out of thee, Ply - - mouth, thee— thee, Al - ba - ny,—
Full Chorus.
p
Bass 1. 2.
Win - ter
tr
p
Ped.

Full Chorus.
A - way!
Ye burn: a - - way!
Full Chorus.
A - way!
Ye burn: a - way!
cries, Ye freeze:......... Fe - ver cries,........................ Hun - ger
Ped.
Ye starve: a - way! Ven - - geance cries, Your
Ye starve: a - way! Ven - - geance cries, Your
cries........................
rall.
C. B. Vcelli. Fag.

Adagio Molto.
Allegro come prima.
graves shall stay!
D
graves shall stay!
Adagio Molto.
Allegro come prima.
poco accel.
Then old Shapes and Masks of Things,
Then old Shapes and Masks of Things,
8ves ad lib.

Framed like Faiths or clothed as Kings, War, and his most noi - sy
Framed like Faiths or clothed as Kings, War, and his most noi - sy
lords, Tongued with lithe and poi - soned swords,
lords, Tongued with lithe and poi - soned swords,

ff
Er - ror, Ter - ror, Rage and Crime, All.... in a win - dy
ff
Er - ror, Ter - ror, Rage and Crime, All.... in a win - dy
ff
sf
night of time, Cried to me from land and sea, "No!...........
sf
night of time, Cried to me from land and sea, "No!...........
sf sf sf sf
Ped. * Ped. *

sf
No!............ Thou shalt not be!"
sf
No!............ Thou shalt not be!"
sff
sf
sf
mp
Ped.
pp
sotto voce.
E
Hark! Hark! Hu-guenots whispering
pp
sotto voce.
Hark! Hark! Hu-guenots whispering
L. H.
pp
Ped.

pp sotto voce.
Hark! Hark!
yea, yea, yea in the dark,
pp sotto voce.
Hark! Hark!
yea, yea, yea in the dark,
Ped. Ped.
Pu - ritans an - swering yea, yea, yea in the dark,
Pu - ritans an - swering yea, yea, yea in the dark,

Yea,..... like an ar - row shot true to his mark, Darts thro' the ty - rannous
Yea,..... like an ar - row shot true to his mark, Darts thro' the ty - rannous
heart of De - ni - al. Pa - tience and La - bor and sol - emn-souled Tri - al,
heart of De - ni - al. Pa - tience and La - bor and sol - emn-souled Tri - al,
pizz.
arco.

mf
p
Foiled, still be - gin - ning, Soiled, but not sin - ning, Toil thro' the ster-torous
mf
p
Foiled, still be - gin - ning, Soiled, but not sin - ning, Toil thro' the ster-torous
Cor.
Clar. Fag. Eng. H.
p Tromboni.
Str.
(Wind sustain.)
death of the Night, Toil, when wild broth-er-wars new - dark the Light, Toil, and for -
f
death of the Night, Toil, when wild broth-er-wars new - dark the Light, Toil, and for -
sf

p
give, and kiss o'er and re - plight.
p
F
give, and kiss o'er, and re - plight.
pizz.
p
Ped. sempre. mp
Ped.
mf
Now Praise to God's oft-
mf
Now Praise to God's oft-
cres.

f cres.
grant - ed grace, Now Praise to Man's un - daunt - ed
f cres.
grant - ed grace, Now Praise to Man's un - dauut - ed
cres.
f
face, De - spite the land, de - spite the
f
face, De - spite the land, de - - - - spite the
f
Ped. sempre.

mf
sea, I was: I am: and I.... shall be,— O how long?
p
sea, I was: I am: and I.... shall be—How long, Good Angel, O how long?
How long, Good An-gel,.... O how long?
sf
p
Corni.
Ped.
Ped.
f
Sing me from Heav'n a man's own song!
f
Sing me from Heav'n a man's own song!
Trombe.
f
p
Tromboni.
8ves
Ped.

G
English Horn Solo.
mf
p
rall. con espress.
pizz.
8ves.
Poco piu Lento.
Bass Solo.
"Long as thine Art shall love true
Poco piu Lento.
Eng. Horn Obligato.
love, Long as thy Sci - ence, thy Sci - ence truth shall
Ob.
Vcelli.
E. H.
Ped.
Ped.

know, Long as thine Ea - gle harms no Dove,
Eng. H.
Long as thy Law by law shall grow,
Ped.
cres.
ff
Long as thy God is God a - bove,
f
Ped.
Ped.
Thy broth - er ev' - ry man, ev' - ry man be - low,
p
Cor.
Ped.

cres. e poco a poco rallentando.
So long, dear Land, dear Land of all my love, Thy name shall
cres. e poco à poco rallentando.
Ped.
tempo.
shine, thy fame shall glow,... ...... thy fame shall shine!........ .. ..
f tempo.
in tempo.
Dear Land, dear Land of all.... ....
colla voce.
Eng. H.
Clar. Fag. p
Str. pizz.
Eng. Horn.
my love.
pp
tempo.
cres. molto.

ff
Allegro Maestoso.
O Mu - - sic, from this height of
time my Word un - fold;
ff
O Mu - - sic, from this height of
time my Word un - fold;
Allegro Maestoso.
ff

In thy large sig - - - nals all men's
In thy large sig - - - nals all men's
hearts Man's Heart................ be - hold:...............
hearts Man's Heart................ be - hold:...............

H
ff With Energy
Mid - heaven un - roll, un - roll........ thy chords as friend - ly flags un -
sf
sf
ff
Mid - heaven un - roll,...... un - roll........ thy chords as
furled, And wave................ the world's best lov - er's wel - come to the

ff
Mid - heaven un - roll,........ un - roll......... thy
friendly flags un - furled, And wave.............. the world's best lov - er's wel - come
world. Mid-heaven...... un - roll................ thy chords, un - roll thy
ff
Mid - heaven un - roll, un -
chords as friend-ly flags un - furled, And wave.............. the world's best
to the world, And wave the world's best lov - - - er's wel-come
chords as friendly flags un - furled, the world's best lov - er's wel - - come

roll...... thy chords as friendly flags un-furled, And wave.............. the
lov - er's wel - - come, wel - come to the world. Un-
to the world. Mid-heav'n un - roll, un - - roll........ thy chords, unto the world.
world's best lov-er's wel - come, the world's best lov - er's wel-come, wel - - come
roll....................... thy chords, un - roll thy chords..........
roll........ thy chords,.............. un - roll thy chords, un - roll thy
Mid - heaven un - roll, un - roll........ thy chords as

to the world,........ And wave the world's best lover's wel - come, the world's best lov-er's
.....: as friend - - ly flags un - - furled,............. as
chords as friendly flags un - . furled, Mid - heaven un - roll, un-
friend-ly flags un - furled, And wave the world's............. best lov - er's wel - come to the
wel - come, her welcome to the world !
flags un - furled, Mid - heaven un - roll, un-roll...... thy
rall........ thy chords...... as friend-ly flags, as friend - ly flags un-
world, her wel-come to ..... the world. Mid-heaven un - roll............

poco stringendo.
Mid - heaven un - roll, un - roll........ thy chords..... as friend - ly flags un -
chords, un - roll............. thy chords as friend - - ly
poco stringendo.
furled, un - roll, un - roll thy chords.... as friend - ly flags un -
.... thy chords as friendly flags, as friend - ly flags un - furled, as friend - - ly
poco stringendo.
furled, And wave the world's best lov - er's wel - come, wel - - - - -
flags un-furled, And wave the world's best lov - er's wel - come,
furled, And wave the world's best lov - er's wel - come, wel - - - - -
flags un - furled, And wave the world's best lov - er's wel - come,
8va..................

sf
- - come, wel - - come to the world,..............................
sf
- - come, wel - - come to the world,..............................
ff L.H.
3 Trumpets.
Ped.
sf
......
wel - - - come!
sf
......
wel - - - come!
3 Trombones.
sf Tutti.

sf
wel - - - - - - come!
sf
wel - - - - - - come!
8va
sempre marcato.
sff
Ped.
8va. bassa.

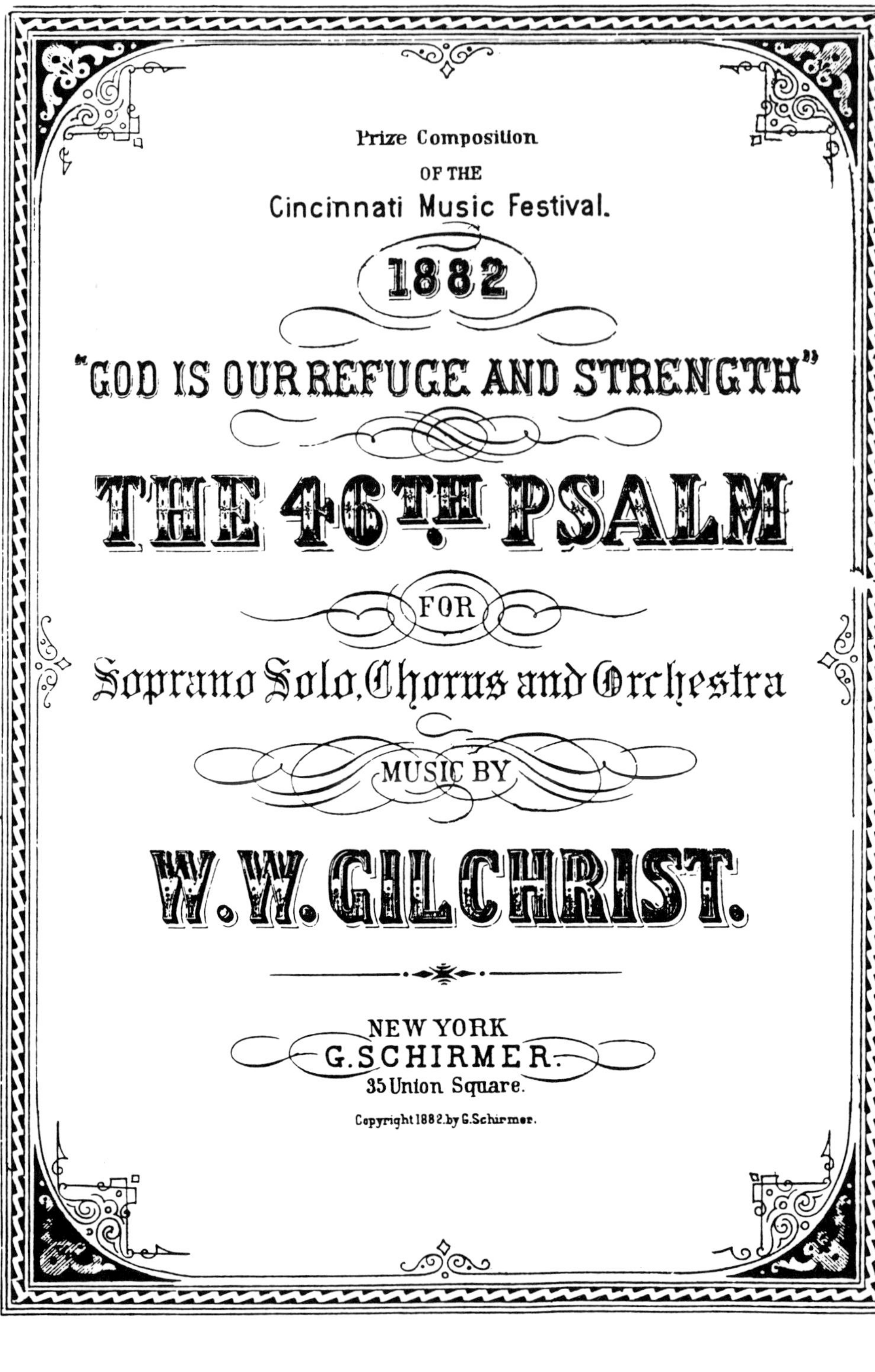

Prize Composition

OF THE

Cincinnati Music Festival.

1882

"GOD IS OUR REFUGE AND STRENGTH"

THE 46TH PSALM

FOR

Soprano Solo, Chorus and Orchestra

MUSIC BY

W. W. GILCHRIST.

NEW YORK

G. SCHIRMER.

35 Union Square.

THE FORTY SIXTH PSALM.

W. W. GILCHRIST.

2877

cresc. poco a poco.
dim.
Ped.
cre - - scen - - do.
8
3.A
ff
f
Più mosso.
cre - - scen - - do.
L.H.
mp

cresc.
p
f
f
dim.
p
pp
5.
Tempo I.
ad lib.
6.
Allegro moderato e maestoso.
fp
poco - a - poco - cre - - scen - - do.
8vs
8vs

f
ff p
cresc.
mf
cresc.
f
cresc.
ff
ff
ff
8

9.
Ped.
Ped.
Ped.
Ped.
Ped.
SOP. Un poco meno mosso, ma molto maestoso. (♩= 120.)
God is our re-fuge and strength,
God is our re-fuge and
ALTO.
TUTTI.
TEN.
God is our re-fuge and strength,
God is our re-fuge and
BASS.
Un poco meno mosso, ma molto maestoso. (♩= 120.)
Ped.

strength
God is our
strength
God is our re - fuge
God is our re - fuge
God is our re - fuge, our re - fuge and
re - fuge
God is our
God is our re - fuge, our re - fuge and
God is our re - fuge and strength, is our
strength.
strength.
9

sempre legato
A ve-ry present help in trou-ble
sempre legato.
A ve-ry present help in trou-ble
sempre legato
a ve-ry present
Un più mosso. (♩=138.)
sf
107
a ve-ry present help
a ve-ry present help
a ve-ry
help
a ve-ry present help
a ve-ry present
a ve-ry present help in trou-ble, God is our
pres- ent
help in trou- ble, God is our
a help in trou-ble, God is our re-fuge

strength God is our strength,
God is our strength, our
strength God is our strength, God is our
God is our re - fuge and strength,
God is our strength, God is our re -
strength, our strength, God is our re -
strength, God is our strength, God is our re -
- fuge a ve-ry present help in trou - ble a ve-ry present
fuge and strength our strength
fuge and strength a ve-ry present help

help in trou - ble a ve - ry present help in trou -
a present help, help
a ve - ry present help, help in trou -
a ve - ry present help in trou -
11
ble
There - fore will we not
ble
There - fore will we not
Allegro molto e con fuoco. (♩ = 184.)
11
fear tho' the earth be re - mov - ed, Tho' the moun - tains be
fear tho' the earth be re - mov - ed, Tho' the moun - tains be

car - ried in - to the midst of the sea, tho' the moun - tains be
car - ried in - to the midst of the sea, tho' the moun - tains be
car - ried in - to the midst of the sea. Therefore will we not
car - ried in - to the midst of the sea. Therefore will we not
sea. Therefore will we not fear,
fear, Therefore will we not fear, Tho' the moun - tains be
fear, There - fore will we not fear tho' the
Therefore will we not fear

car - ried in - to the midst of the sea.
Tho' the moun - tains be car - ried in - to the
earth be re - mov - ed. Tho' the moun - tains be car - ried in - to the
12
midst of the sea.
God is our re - fuge God is our
midst of the sea. God is our re - fuge God is our
God is our re - fuge God is our strength
12
re - fuge, God is our re - fuge and strength our
re - fuge, God is our re - fuge and strength our
God is our re - fuge

ff
re - fuge ——— There - fore will we not fear tho' the earth be re -
our strength Therefore will we not fear tho' the
re - fuge ——— our strength
ff
mov - ed Tho' the moun - tains be
earth be re - mov - ed
There - fore will we not fear tho' the earth be re - mov - ed
Therefore will we not fear There - fore will we not
13
car - ried in - to the midst of the sea Therefore will we not
Tho' the moun - tains be car - ried in - to the sea
fear Tho' the earth be re - mov - ed
13

fear There-fore will we not fear We will not fear, tho' the
There-fore will we not fear There-fore will we not fear, tho' the
tho' the
fff
earth be re - mov - ed and the moun-tains are car-ried, are carried in - to the midst of the sea are car-ried in - to the
in
to the midst, the midst of the sea
earth be re - mov - ed the mountains are car - ried, car - ried in - to the midst of the sea are car-ried in - to the
earth be re - mov - ed are carried in - to the sea
mf
molto cre - scen - do.
trem.

midst the midst of the sea to the midst of the
midst the midst of the sea to the midst of the
the midst of the sea
14 sea.
Tho' the waves there-of roar
sea.
Tho' the waves there-of roar
14
Furioso.
ff
sf
14
Tho' the waves there-of roar
Tho' the
Tho' the waves there-of roar
Tho' the

waves thereof roar and be trou - - - bled And the mountains
waves thereof roar and be trou - - - bled And the mountains
Tho' the waves
shake with the swell -, ing there - of. Tho' the waves
shake with the swell - ing there - of.
Tho the mountains shake
15
15
roar Tho' the waves roar And the mountains
Tho' the waves roar Tho' the waves roar

shake
And the mountains shake
Tho' the
And the mountains shake
And the mountains shake
Tho' the
mf
waves there-of
roar
And the
waves there-of
roar
And the
mf
moun - tains
shake.
moun - tains
shake.
f

16
Tho' the waves there-of
16
Tho' the waves there-of
16
roar
Tho' the mountains shake
roar
Tho' the mountains shake
Tho' the mountains shake
with the swelling there-
Tho' the mountains shake
with the swelling there-

ff
of
With the
ff
ff
of
With the
ff
ff
17
swell - ing there - of
A very present help in trou-ble
ing
swell - ing there - of
God is our re - fuge and strength our
swell - ing there - of
God is our
f
17
God is our re - fuge and strength our re - fuge and
A very present help
God is our re - fuge and
re - fuge and strength
A very present help
re - fuge and strength
A very present help in
f

strength A very present help in trou - ble A very present help in trouble
strength God is our strength
God is our re - fuge God is our strength God is our
trouble God is our re - fuge and strength
L.H.
A very present help in trou - ble Therefore will we not
re - fuge God is our strength Therefore will we not
God is our re - fuge and strength
L.H.
18
fear tho' the earth be re - mov - ed
fear tho' the earth be re - mov - ed
Therefore will we not fear tho' the earth be re - mov'd
legato
18

cresc. poco a poco
molto cre - scen - do.
19
ff
Therefore will we not fear tho' the earth be re - mov - ed tho' the
Therefore will we not fear tho' the earth be re - mov - ed tho' the
mountains be car - ried in-to the midst of the sea
mountains be car - ried in-to the midst of the sea

Tho' the waves thereof roar— and be trou - bled
roar— and be trou - bled
Tho' the waves thereof
Tho' the moun-tains shake— with the dwel - ling there - of.
shake— with the dwel - ling there - of.
Tho' the moun-tains
God is our re - fuge God
God is our re - fuge God

ff
is our re - - fuge
20 God is our re - - fuge our
ff
ff
is our re - - fuge
God is our re - - fuge our
ff
and
molto cre - scen - do.
ff
20
string.
re - - fuge and strength
God is our re - fuge
re - - fuge and strength
God is our re - fuge
strength
God is our re - fuge
God is our
string.
L.H.
ff
God is our strength
a ve - ry present help in trou - ble.
ff
God is our strength
a ve - ry present help in trou - ble.
strength
L.H.

fp
rall. poco a poco.
p
p
Ped.
21
SOPR. SOLO. tranquillo.
There is a riv - er the
Andante contempletif. (♩= 66.)
stream whereof shall make glad the ci - ty of God A riv - - er the
22
stream whereof shall make glad the ci-ty of God The holy place of the
23

cresc.
dwelling of the Most High
24.
The ho - ly
Ped.
place of the dwel - ling of the Most High!
f appass.
God is in the midst of her God is in the midst of her She shall
dim.
not be mov - ed God is in the midst of her God is in the
25.
midst of her she shall not be mov - -

ed
26.
There is a riv - er the stream where-of shall make
There is a riv - er the stream where-of shall make
Violin
26.
glad the ci-ty of God a riv - - er the
a riv - er the
glad the ci-ty of God a riv - - er the
The
27.
27.

The holy place of the
stream whereof shall make glad the city of God The holy
stream whereof shall make
stream whereof shall make glad the city of God The holy
stream where of shall make glad
28
tabernacle
place of the dwelling of the Most High.
place of the dwelling of the Most High.
The
29
cresc.

ho - ly place of the taber- nacle
80
The holy place of the dwelling of
The ho - ly place of the
of the dwel - ling
tr
30
appass.
God is in the midst of her
the Most High!
God is in the
dwel - ling of the Most High
God is in the
of the Most High.
p
f

Più mosso
God is in the midst of her, She shall not be mov - ed
midst of her, in the midst of her God shall
midst of her, in the midst of her God shall
Più mosso.

cresc.
appass.
a tempo.
God shall help her, God shall help her God shall help her and that right
31
help her, God shall help her God shall help her, God shall
help her, God shall help her God shall help her, God shall
a tempo.
col voce.
31

ear-ly God shall help her and that right
82
ear-ly,
poco accel.
help her
God shall
poco accel.
help her
God shall
col voce.
poco accel.
82
poco accel.
God shall help her God shall help her shall help her and
help her God shall help her
help her God shall help her
a tempo.
a tempo.

that right ear - - ly,
God shall help her and that right ear -
help her and
God shall help her and that right ear -
p
33
God shall help her, God shall help her and that right ear -
ly, God shall help her, God shall help
ly, God shall help her, God shall help
God shall help
p
pp
poco rall.

34
35 Allegro molto.
ly.
her.
The heathen rag'd
her.
The heathen rag'd
Allegro molto.
tr
p
molto tranquillo.
attacca.
f
Ped.
The nations were mov'd,
He utter'd his voice the earth
melted.
The nations were mov'd,
He utter'd his voice the earth
melted.
The heathen rag'd,
The nations were mov'd,
He utter'd his voice the earth
The heathen rag'd,
The nations were mov'd,
He utter'd his voice the earth

melted, The hea — then rag'd — the nations were mov - ed,
melted, The hea — then rag'd — the nations were mov -
He utter'd his voice the earth melted.
The hea - then rag'd — the nations were mov -
ed, He utter'd his voice the earth melted.
The hea — then rag'd — the nations were mov - ed,
The heathen rag'd, the heathen rag'd,
ed, He utter'd his voice the earth melted, The heathen rag'd, the nations were
The heathen rag'd, the nations were
He utter'd his voice the earth melted,

The nations were mov'd, He uter'd his voice the earth melted, The
mov'd,
mov'd, He ut-ter'd his voice the earth melted, The
86
Lord our God is with us, The God of Ja-cob is our re-fuge, The
Lord our God is with us, The God of Ja-cob is our re-fuge, The
Lord our God is with us The God of Ja-cob is our re-fuge.
Lord our God is with us The God of Ja-cob is our re-fuge. The

The
Lord of hosts is with us, The God of Ja - cob is our
The
Lord of hosts is with us. The God of Ja - cob is our
re - fuge The Lord of hosts is with us, is
Lord of hosts is with us. The God of Ja - cob is our re - fuge.
re - fuge. The Lord of hosts is with us. Our re - fuge,
with us. The God of Ja - cob is our re - fuge. Our
The Lord of hosts is

37
our re - fuge.
Come be - hold the works of the
re - fuge.
Come
with us, The God of Ja - cob is our re-fuge.
Lord,
Come be - hold the works of the Lord,
Come be - hold the works of the Lord,
Come be -
What deso - la - tions in
What deso - la - tions He hath made
hold the works of the Lord, What deso - la - tions in
He hath made.

all the earth, What des-o - lations He hath made in all the earth
cresc.
all the earth, What des-o - lations He hath made in all the earth
The Lord of hosts is
L. H.
38
The Lord of hosts is
The Lord is with us The Lord is with us
The Lord is with us The Lord is with us
with us. The God of Ja - cob is our re - fuge
with us The God of Ja - cob is our refuge Be -
The Lord is with us The Lord is with us
The Lord is with us Come be-hold the works of the

hold the works of the Lord
Be - hold the works of the
Lord
Come
be - hold the works of the Lord
ff
Lord, Come, be - hold the works of the
The
Come, be - hold the works of the Lord
89
ff
The Lord of hosts is with us. The God of Ja - cob is our
f
Lord of hosts is with us. The God of Ja - cob is our re - fuge
The Lord of hosts is with us. The God of Ja - cob is our
f
ff
89

refuge Come be - hold the works of the
Come be - hold the works of the Lord
refuge Come be - hold the works of the
Lord What des-o - la - tions
What des-o - la - tions he hath
Lord What des-o - la - tions
What des - o - la-tions he hath made, hath made in all the
he hath made, What des-o - lations he hath made in all the earth in all the
made,
he hath made What des-o - lations he hath made in all the earth in all the
earth,

40
earth The heathen rag'd The nations were mov'd He ut-ter'd his
earth. The heathen rag'd The nations were mov'd He ut-ter'd his voice the earth
40
voice the earth melted The heathen rag'd The nations were
melted The heathen rag'd The nations were mov'd
mov'd He ut-ter'd his voice the earth melted The
He ut-ter'd his voice the earth melted The Lord our God is

Lord our God is with us, is with us The God of
The Lord of hosts is with us The God of Jacob is our refuge
with us The Lord of hosts is with us The Lord of hosts is
The God of
Ja-cob is our re-fuge The Lord of hosts is
our re-fuge
with us the God of Ja-cob is our re-fuge The Lord of hosts is
Ja-cob is our re-fuge
with us the God of Ja-cob is our re-fuge.
with us the God of Ja-cob is our re-fuge.
with us
L.H.
dim.
R.H.

SOPR. SOLO.
41
He maketh wars to cease in all the earth, He breaketh the bow
L'istesso tempo.
legato.
pp
41
and knappeth the spear in sun-der He maketh wars to cease in all the
earth He breaketh the bow, and knap-peth the spear in sun-
42
TUTTI.
der. He maketh wars to cease, to cease in all the
He maketh wars to cease
42

SOLO.
earth
He maketh wars to cease in all the
to cease in all the earth
Ped.
TUTTI.
earth, He breaketh, he breaketh the bow, And
He breaketh, he break - eth the
knap-peth the spear in sun - der He breaketh, he break-eth the
SOLO.
bow And knap - peth the spear in sun - der

bow. And knappeth the spear in sun-der He knappeth the spear in
43
sun - der He burn - eth the cha - riot with fire
He burn-eth the cha - riot with
He burn-eth the cha - riot with
43
SOLO.
fire. He mak - eth wars to cease in all the
fire.
legato

earth He break-eth, he breaketh the bow And knappeth the spear in
sunder. He breaketh, he breaketh the
He maketh wars to cease in all the earth He
He maketh wars to cease in all the earth He
fp
44
bow And knap-peth the spear in sun - der and
break-eth, he break-eth the bow And knap-peth the spear in
break-eth, he break-eth the bow And knap-peth the spear in
44

burn - - - - eth the cha - riot And burn - eth the cha - riot with
sun - der And
sun - der And
fire And burn - - - eth the cha - riot, the cha - riot with
burneth the cha - riot with fire
burneth the cha - riot with fire

fire
The hea-then rag'd The na-tions were
The hea-then rag'd
The na-tions were mov'd
mov'd He ut-ter'd his voice the earth melt-ed
He ut-ter'd his voice the earth melt-ed
The hea-then rag'd The na-tions were
The hea-then rag'd
The na-tions were mov'd

45
mov'd the nations were mov'd the earth melt-ed The
The na-tions were mov'd the earth melted The
Lord of hosts is with us The God of Ja-cob is our re-fuge The
Lord of hosts is with us The God of Ja-cob is our re-fuge The
46
Lord of hosts is with us The God of Ja-cob is our re-fuge,
47
Lord of hosts is with us Come be-
The God of Ja-cob in our re-fuge,

Come be - hold the works of the Lord.
hold the works of the Lord
Come be -
Come be - hold the works of the Lord.
Come be - hold the works of the Lord What des-o -
hold the works of the Lord.
What des-o -
Come
What des-o - lations he hath
dim.
la - tions he hath made He hath made in all the earth. He maketh
la - tions
la - tions he hath made He hath made in all the earth.
made What des-o - lations he hath made in all the earth.
SOLO
p legato.

wars to cease in all the earth.
He breaketh the bow
And knappeth the spear in sun-der
He mak-eth wars to cease in
all the earth.
He breaketh the bow and knappeth the spear in sun-
49
TUTTI.
der. He maketh wars to cease
to cease in all the
TUTTI. He maketh wars to cease
49

SOLO. legato.
earth.
He maketh wars to cease in all the
to cease in all the earth.
earth He mak-eth wars to cease in all the earth He
50
breaketh, he breaketh the bow and knap-peth the spear in
He break-eth, he break-eth the bow. And
He break-eth, he break-eth the bow. And
50

sun - der And burn - - - eth the cha - riot and
knap - peth the spear in sun - der.
knap - peth the spear in sun - der.
burn - eth the cha - riot with fire And burn - - -
And burn - eth the cha - riot with fire
And burn - eth the cha - riot with fire

eth the cha - riot, the cha - riot with fire
He
He knappeth the spear in
knappeth the spear in sun - der He knappeth the spear in
sun - der He knappeth the spear in sun - der
sunder He burneth the chariot the chariot with
He burn - eth the chariot the chariot with fire with

51
fire.
fire.
51
p
Be still then Be still then and know that I am
ritard. dim.
God.
God.
Andante con espressivo.
Andante con espressivo.
sf
dim.
p
ritard.

52
p
Be still then
p
p
Be still then
p
52
53
pp
Be still then
pp
pp
Be still then
pp
54
And
And
53
54
know_ that I am God.
know_ that I am God.
fp
dim

55
I am God, God.
I am God, God.
appass.
I will be exalted Ex-
I will be exalted Ex-
alted in all the earth.
alted in all the earth.

Ex - alt - ed in all the earth
Be still then, Be
Ex - alt - ed
Ex - alt - ed in all the earth
Be still then, Be
Be still then Be still then
56
still and know that I am God,
and know that I am
rall.
still and know that I am God,
and know that I am
The
rall.
52 Allegro molto e maestoso. (𝅗𝅥 = 152.)
God.
The
God.
The God of Jacob is our re -
marcato.
Lord of hosts is with us. The God of Ja-cob is our re -
Allegro molto e maestoso. (𝅗𝅥 = 152.)
marcato.
52

The God of Ja-cob is our
Lord of hosts is with us. The God of Ja-cob is our
fuge The Lord of hosts is with us, The Lord is
fuge The Lord is with us,
re - fuge The Lord of hosts is with us, The
with us, is
with us. The Lord of hosts is
The Lord of hosts is with us, The God of Ja-cob is our
58
Lord of hosts is with us,
with us, is with us, The God of
with us, is with us, The Lord is with us,
re - fuge The Lord of hosts is with us,
58

ff
The God of Ja-cob is our re - - fuge The
Jacob is our re - - fuge The Lord is with
ff
The Lord of hosts is with us. The
The Lord of hosts is with us. The Lord of hosts
tr
59
mf cre -
God of Jacob is our re - - fuge. The Lord of
us. The Lord is with us. The Lord is
cre
Lord The Lord is with us. The Lord of hosts
mf
is with us the Lord is with us.
mf cre - - scen -
59
- - scen - - do.
hosts is with us. The Lord of hosts is with us.
scen - - - do.
is with us. The Lord of hosts is with us.
The Lord of
- - - do.

60
The Lord of hosts, of hosts is with us. The Lord of hosts,
The Lord of hosts, of hosts is with us. The Lord of hosts,
Lord of hosts, of hosts is with us. The God of Ja - cob is our
60
of hosts is with us, is with us, The God of Ja - cob is our
of hosts is with us, is with us, The God of Ja - cob is our
re - fuge The Lord of hosts is with us,
61
re - fuge. The God of Ja-cob is our
The Lord of hosts is with us The God of
re - - fuge. our
The Lord of hosts is with us
61

re - fuge.
The Lord of hosts is with us
The God of Ja-cob is our
re fuge.
The Lord of hosts
re - fuge.
The God of Ja-cob is our
The Lord of hosts is with us
re - fuge the Lord
62
The Lord of hosts
is with
re - fuge the Lord
The Lord of hosts
is with
The Lord of hosts is with us, the Lord of hosts is with
62
us, The Lord of hosts The Lord is with us The Lord of
63
us, The Lord of hosts The Lord is with us
us The Lord, the Lord of hosts
63

cresc.
ff
64
hosts is with us. The Lord of hosts is with us The Lord of
cresc.
is with us. is with us The Lord of
ff
cresc.
cresc.
Brass
ff
64
hosts is with us, the Lord is with us. The
ff
hosts is with us, the Lord is with us. The
ff
ff
Lord of hosts the Lord of hosts is with us.
Lord of hosts
Lord of hosts the Lord of hosts is with us.
the Lord is with us.
Ped.

65
Glo - ry
Glo - ry
Glo - ry
Glo - ry
65
Fa - ther
Glo - ry be to the Fa - ther
Fa - ther
Glo - ry be to the Fa - ther
Fa - ther
Fa - ther
L.H.
R.H.
66
To the Fa - ther and to the Son, and
To the Fa - ther
To the Fa - ther, and to the Son
più mosso.
66

to the Son to the Father and to the Son
and to the Son and to the Son
To the Father and to the Son to the Son
and to the Son
and to the Holy Ghost
and to the Holy Ghost
As it
As it was in the be-
As it was in the be-gin-ning is
As it was in the be-gin-ning is now and
was in the be-gin-ning is now, is
gin-ning is now and ev-er shall be
67

now, now and ev - er shall be
ev - er shall be world with - out end world with - out end,
now and ev - er shall be world with - out end, A -
as it was in the be - gin - - ning is now and
68
world with - out end A - -
A - - men, a - - - men, as it
- men, as it was in the be - gin - ning
ev - er shall be world with - out end, world
68
- men a - - - - men is now and ev - er
was in the be - ginning is now and ev - er shall be
is now and ev - er shall be
with - - out end world

69
shall be world without end, world without end
The
The Lord of hosts is with us
with-out end world with-out end.
69
world with-out end A-
God of Ja-cob is our re-fuge, A-men
is our re-fuge, A-
The Lord of hosts is with
men.
The Lord our God is
70
a-men, a-
men a-men, The Lord, the
us, the God of Ja-cob is our re-fuge, The Lord of
70
Ped.

with __ us, the God of Ja - cob is our re - - fuge. The Lord ___
men a - - - men. The
Lord of hosts, of hosts is with __ us. The Lord ___
hosts ___ is with ___ us. ___
— of hosts ___ is with ___ us, A - -
— of hosts ___ is with ___ us, A - -
SOLO. TUTTI. SOLO.
men a - men, a - men, a - men.
SOLO. TUTTI. SOLO.
men a - men, a - men, a - men.
SOLO. TUTTI. SOLO.

ff TUTTI.
Glo - ry be to the Fa - - ther and to the Son and to the Ho - ly Ghost,
ff
TUTTI.
ff
Glo - ry be to the Fa - - ther and to the Son and to the Ho - ly Ghost,
ff
and to the Ho ly Ghost,
71
As it was in the be - gin - ning
As it was in the be - gin - ning
ff
72
is now and ev - er shall be World
is now and ev - er shall be World

78
with - out end A - men, a - men, a - men, a - men,
with - out end A - men, a - men, a - men, a - men,
73

accel.
a tempo.
ff
accel.
World without end, A - - men.
ff
a tempo.
accel.
accel.
World without end, A - - men.
ff
accel.
a tempo.
accel.
ff
accel.
a tempo.
accel.

a tempo.
A - - men.
a tempo.
A - - men.
a tempo.
a tempo.
stringendo.

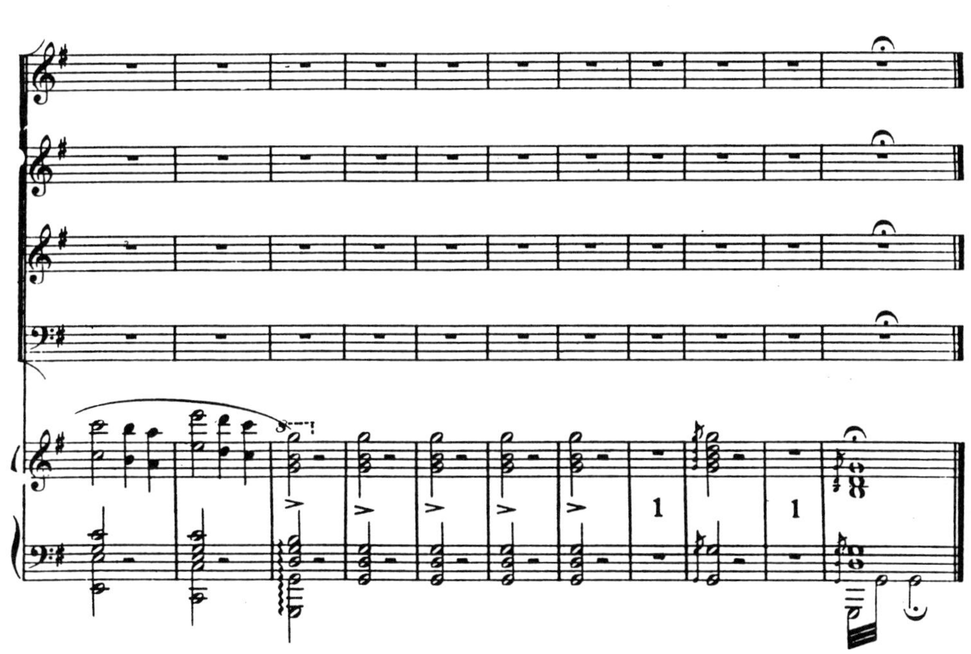
1
1

in E flat

composed
by

Mrs. H. H. A. Beach.

VOCAL SCORE

with Pianoforte Accompaniment

arranged from the Full Score.

BOSTON:

ARTHUR P. SCHMIDT.

Kyrie.

Organ, Strings, Wood Wind & 2 Horns.

A. P. S. 2637

Boston: Arthur P. Schmidt.

Più mosso. (♩= 63.)
pp rit.
p SOLO
son, e - lei-son, e-lei - son. Ky - - - ri-e e-lei-son,
Ky - rie e-lei-son, e-le-i - son.
e e - lei-son, e-le-i - son.
Ky - rie e-lei-son, e-lei - son.
Più mosso. (♩= 63.)
Fl.
rit.
Organo tacet
pp
Cl. & Bassn.
CHORUS
mf
f
Kyrie e - leison, Ky - ri - e, Ky - ri - e e - le-i -
Ky - ri - e e - le - i - son, Ky - ri - e, Ky - ri -
Ky - rie e - le - i - son, Ky - ri - e, Ky - ri -
Ky - ri - e, Ky - ri -
Str. & Wood
son, e - le-i - son.
SOLO
e e - le-i - son. Ky - - - ri-e e - lei-son, Kyrie e - lei-son,
e e - le-i - son.
e e - lei - son.
pp
Str.
p

CHORUS
Ky - ri - e — e - lei - son,
Ky - ri - e, Ky - ri - e, Ky - ri - e — e - le - i - son,
Ky - ri - e,
Ky - ri - e, Ky - ri - e,
Ky - ri -
Ky - ri - e, Ky - ri - e, Ky - ri - e e - le - i - son, e -
Str. & Wood
cresc.
dolce
Ky - rie e - le - i - son.
Ky - rie e - le - i - son.
e e - le - i - son.
lei - son, e - le - i - son.
Christe e -
Horns
Celli
Str. & Wood
lei - son, e - le - i - son. Chri - ste e - lei - son, e -
Fl.
Viol.

le - i - - son, Christe e - le-i-son, e - le - i - son.
SOLO
le - - - i - son, Christe e - lei - son, e - lei - son. Chri -
lei - son, e - lei - son, Christe e - lei - son, e - le - i - son.
lei - son, e - le - - - i - son, Chri - ste e - lei - - son.
Cl.
cresc.
Bassn. & Str.
Str.
Celli
Bassi
SOLO
Chri - - ste,
ste e - lei - - son, Chri - - ste,
SOLO
Chri - - ste e - le - - i - son,
SOLO
Chri - - ste e - lei - son,
cresc.
Chri - ste e - lei - - son, Chri - ste e - lei - son,
CHORUS
Chri - ste e -
Viol.
Horn & Wood

lei - - son, e lei - - son, e - le - i - son,
SOLO
Ky -
Cl. & Horn
Horn
pp
Str.
Str. & Bassn.
ri - e e - le - i - son.
CHORUS
Ky - ri - e e - lei - - son,
Ky - ri - e e -
più cresc.
Wood Wind & Horns
Ky - ri - - - e, Ky-rie e - lei - son, e - lei - son,
cresc.
lei - son, Ky - ri - e,
e - le - i - son,
Cl. & Horn
Tutti

mf
cresc.
f
Ky - ri - e, Ky - ri - e e - - le - - i - son. Ky -
Ky - - ri - e e - le - i - son, e - le - - i - son, Ky - ri -
Ky - - ri - e e - le - i - son e - le - - i - - son, Ky - - ri -
Ky - - ri - e e - le - i - son, e - lei - - - son,
Cl. & Fl.
p Str.
cresc.
Horn
dim.
Str. & Wood
dolce
pp
- - ri - e e - le - i - son, e - le - i -
e - e - lei - son, e - le - i - son, e - le - i -
e e - le - - - - i - son, e - le - i -
e - lei - son, e - le - i - son, e - le - i -
Ob. & Cl.
p Str.
Celli
son.
son.
son.
son.
Viol. con sordini
Fl.
Ob.
Cl.
R.H.
sempre pp
Str.

Gloria.

Wood Wind, Strings, 4 Horns, 3 Trombones, 3 Trumpets & Kettle Drum.

CHORUS
Glo-ri-a_in ex-celsis De - - o, in_ex - cel - - - sis De - -
Glo-ri-a_in ex-celsis De - - o, in ex - cel - sis De - -
Glo-ri-a_in ex-celsis De - - o, in_ex - cel-sis, in ex - cel - -
Glo-ri-a_in ex-celsis De - - o, in ex - cel - sis De - -
Str. arco
Wind
f Trpts. & Horns
Horns
Trpts. & Wind
o. Glo - ri - a in ex - cel-sis De-o, in ex - cel - - - sis
o. Glo - ri - a in ex - cel-sis De-o, in ex - cel - - - sis
sis. Glo - ri - a in ex - cel-sis De-o, in ex - cel - - - sis,
o. Glo - ri - a in ex - cel - sis, Glori - a in ex - cel -
Str. & Clar.
Ob.
Viol.
Bassi & Horn
De - - o, in ex - cel - - sis.
De - - o, in ex - cel - - sis.
in_ ex - cel - - - sis De - - o.
sis, in_ ex - cel - sis De - - o.
Cl.
Trpt. Horn Fl. & Ob.
ff Str. Cl. & Bassn.
Str.
A.P.S. 2637

Glo - ri - a
Glo - ri - a in ex - cel - sis, ex -
Glo - ri - a in ex - cel -
Glo - ri - a in ex -
Wind & Horns
Vl. Ob. & Trp.
Str. & Wind
Bassi
Bassi & Bassns
in ex -
cel - sis, in ex - cel - sis De - o.
cel - sis, in ex - cel sis De - o.
sis, in ex - cel - sis, in ex - cel - sis.
cel - sis, ex - cel - sis, in ex - cel - sis.
cresc.
Str. & Trpts.
Glo - ri - a
Glo - ri - a in ex - cel -
Glo - ri - a in ex -
Glo - ri - a in
Wind
Viol. & Trpt.
Horns
Str. & Wind
Bassi & Bassns.

mf
cresc.
f
in ex - cel - sis, in ex - cel - - - - - sis, in ex-
sis, ex - cel - sis, in ex - cel - - - - sis, in ex-
cel - - - - - sis, in ex - cel - - - sis, ex-cel-
ex - cel - - - - sis, ex - cel - - - - - - sis, in ex-
Viol.
Horns
cel - - - - sis. Glo - ri - a, Glo - ri - a in ex-
ff
Wind
Trpts.
Trombones
Tutti
sempre ff
cel - - - sis.
Fl. & Ob.
ffp
Str
Bassn
coll 8ve

p
Et in ter - ra
poco a poco cresc.
Cl.
f
pp
Str.
Ped.
p
Et in ter - ra pax, ho - mi - nibus, et
cresc.
pax, ho - mi - nibus, ho - mi - ni - bus, et
Bassn.
Cl.
Fl.
Wind cantabile.
ben legato
poco
in ter - ra pax, ho - mi -
in ter - ra pax, ho - mi -
cresc.

A.P.S. 2637

p
- ni - bus, Glori - a in ex - cel - sis De - o,
p
- ni - bus, Glo - ri - a in ex - cel - sis De - o,
p
Et in ter - ra pax, ho -
p
Et in ter - ra, et in ter - ra pax, ho -
Cl.
Viol.
cresc.
pp
Vcl.
dolce
Ped.
mf
f
in ex - cel - sis, bo - nae vo - lun - ta -
in ex - cel - sis, bo - nae vo - lun - ta -
- mi - ni - bus, bo - nae vo - lun ta -
- mi - ni - bus, bo - nae vo - lun - ta -
dim.
Ob.
mf
f
Ped.
mf
tis, bo-nae vo - lun - ta - tis.
tis, bo-nae vo - lun - ta - tis.
tis, bo-nae vo - lun - ta - tis.
tis, vo-lun - ta - tis.
Trpt.
mf
pp
marcato ma pp
Str. pizz.
Ped.
Bassi & Bassn.

A.P.S. 2637

mf
In ex - cel - sis,
Horns Bass & Tromb. sustained.
2nd Vl. arco
Gloria in ex - cel - sis,
in ex -
Gloria in ex - cel - sis,
cel - sis,
Gloria in ex - cel - sis,
in ex - cel - sis,
Gloria in ex-
dim.
1st Vl. arco
2nd Vl.
1st Vl.
cresc.
Wind
Tr. sust.
pp
cel - sis,
Gloria in ex - cel - sis,
in ex - cel - sis,
cel - sis, in excel - sis,
Trpt.
più dim.
Str. pizz.
Cl. & Bassn

in ex - cel - sis De - o,
in ex - cel - sis De - o,
in ex - cel - sis De - o, ex - cel - sis,
in ex - cel - sis, ex - cel - sis,
Vcl. Viola & Bassn.
Fl. Ob. & Clar.
cresc.
Horns
C. B. & Kettle-Drum
De - o, in ex - cel -
Brass.
Tutti
sis De - o, ex -
Trpts
Wind
A. P. S. 2637

cel - - - - - - - - - sis, ex -
Vl.
Trpt. & Horns
dim.
Tromb.
Cl. & Str.
Ped.
cel - - - - sis,
Wind & Str.
pp
Tromb.
f
Trpt. & Horns
Trpt. & Str.
Wind & Horns
Glo - ria in ex - celsis,
in ex cel - - -
in ex -
in
Tutti
ff
p Wind & Str.
A.P.S. 2637

mf
cresc.
f
in — ex - cel - sis, in — ex - cel - - sis De - -
sis, ex - cel - - - sis, in ex - cel - sis De -
cel - - - sis, in ex - cel - - sis De - -
— ex - cel - - - sis, ex - cel - - sis De - -
o, Glo - ri - a in ex -
o, Glo - ri - a in ex -
o, Glo - ri - a in ex -
o,
Trp. & Str.
Wind
Tutti
ff
cel - sis, in — ex - cel - sis,
cel - sis, in — ex - cel - - sis, ex - cel - - sis,
cel - sis, in — ex - cel - - - sis,
in — ex - cel - - -
Wind & Str.
p
cresc.

A.P.S. 2637

in ex - cel - - - - - sis De - - - - - - - o,
in ex - cel - - - - - - sis De - - - - - o,
in ex - cel - - - - - - sis De - - - o,
- - - - sis, in ex-cel - - - - - sis,
Vl.
Horns sustained
Glo-ri-a, Glo-ri-a in ex-cel - - sis.
Glo-ri-a, Glo-ri-a in ex-cel - - sis.
Glo-ri-a, Glo-ri-a in ex-cel - - sis.
Glo-ri-a, Glo-ri-a in ex-cel - - sis.
Tromb.
Fl. & Cl.
Bassn.
Str.
cresc.
A.P.S. 2637

p
Et in ter - ra pax, ho - mi - nibus,
Ob.
Wind & Str.
f
p
Ped.
p
Et in ter - ra pax, ho - mi - nibus, et in
cresc.
et in ter - - - - ra pax, et in
Cl.
Ob.
Cl. & Bassn. 8ve
Bassn.
cresc.
Ped.
p
Et in
pp
dim.
ter - ra pax, ho - mi - ni - bus,
pp
dim.
ter - ra, et in ter - - - ra pax, ho - mi - ni - bus,
dim.
pp Horns
Ped.

Et in ter - - ra, in ter - - ra pax, ho - mi - - ni
ter - - ra, et in ter - ra pax, ho - mi - ni - bus,
Glori-a in ex - cel - sis De - o, in ex - cel - -
Glori-a in ex-cel - - - sis De - o, in ex - cel - - -
Viol.
Viola
Ped.
bus, in ter - ra, et in ter - - ra, in ter - ra
in ter - ra, et in ter - ra pax, in ter - ra,
sis, bonae vo - lun - ta - - tis, bonae
sis, bonae vo - lun - ta - - tis, in ter - ra,
Wind, Str. & Horns
pax, in ter - - ra,
et in ter - - ra,
vo - - - lun ta - - tis,
et in ter - - - ra pax,
Trpt. & Str. pizz.
A.P.S. 2637

ppp
vo - lun - ta - tis,
ppp
vo - lun - ta - tis.
Horns
sempre pp
Ob.
Str.
Ped.
Vcl. & Bassn.
Cl.
K. Drum & C. B.
Fl. & Cl.
Trpt.
poco a poco
Ob.
cresc.
Vcl. & Bassn.
Fl. & Cl.
Cl.
Trpt.
cresc.
Wind, Str. & Horns
Tromb.
Trpts.

f
Glori-a in ex-celsis De - o, in ex - cel - - sis De - o, Glo - ri - a in ex - cel-sis De-o, Glori - a, Glo - ri -
Glori-a in ex-celsis De - o, in ex - cel - sis, Glo - ri - a in ex - cel-sis De-o, Glo - ri -
Glori-a in ex-celsis De - o, in ex - cel - - sis De - o, Glo - ri - a in ex - cel-sis De-o, Glori - a, Glo - ri -
Glori-a in ex-celsis De - o, in ex - cel - sis, Glo - ri - a in ex - cel-sis De-o, Glo - ri -
f Tutti
sempre f
Horns
Trpt. & Ten. Tromb.
ff
ff Tutti
A. P. S. 2637

a, Glo - ri - a in ex - cel - sis De - o,
a, Glo - ri - a in ex - cel - sis De - o,
a, Glo - ri - a in ex - cel - sis De - o,
a, Glo - ri - a in ex - cel - sis De - o,
Trpt. & Ten. Tromb.
ff in ex - cel - sis,
ff in ex - cel - sis De - o,
ff in ex - cel sis De - o,
ff in ex - cel - sis De - o,
ff Tutti
Bassi 8ve
Horn & Tromb.
ff Glo - ri - a, ff Glo - ri - a.
ff Glo - ri - a, ff Glo - ri - a.
ff Glo - ri - a, ff Glo - ri - a.
ff Glo - ri - a, ff Glo - ri - a.
Trpt.
sf Tutti
sf
sf

Selected Bibliography

The bibliography of American sacred music is large and varied. What follows is a selective and subjective listing of items I consider indispensable.

Allen, William Francis, Charles Pickard Ware, and Lucy McKim Garrison. *Slave Songs of the United States.* New York: Agathynian Press, 1867.

Amerigrove. See *The New Grove Dictionary of American Music.*

Appel, Richard G. *The Music of the Bay Psalm Book, 9th Edition (1698).* I.S.A.M. Monographs, no. 5. New York: Institute for Studies in American Music, 1975.

Bandel, Betty. *Sing the Lord's Song in a Strange Land: The Life of Justin Morgan.* Rutherford, N.J.: Fairleigh Dickinson University Press, 1981.

Barbour, J. Murray. *The Church Music of William Billings.* East Lansing: Michigan University Press, 1960.

Barck, Oscar T., and Hugh T. Lefler. *Colonial America*. 2d ed. New York: Macmillan, 1968.

Billings, William. *The New England Psalm Singer.* Boston: printed by Edes and Gill, 1770.

_____. *Singing Master's Assistant.* Boston, Mass.: Printed by Draper and Folsom, 1778.

Block, Adrienne Fried. "Beach, Amy Marcy (Cheney). In *Amerigrove*.

Boroff, Edith. *Music in Europe and the United States: A History.* Englewood Cliff, N.J.: Prentice-Hall, 1971.

Bradford, William. *Of Plymouth Plantation: 1620-1647.* 2 vols. With an introduction by Samuel Eliot Morison. New York: Knopf, 1963.

Britton, Allen P. "Theoretical Introductions in American Tunebooks to 1800." Dissertation, University of Michigan, 1950.

Buechner, Alan. *Notes to "The New England Harmony."* New York: Folkways Records, album no. FA2377, 1964.

Calvin, John. *Genesis*. Translated and edited by John King. Edinburgh: Banner of Truth Trust, 1965.

_____. *Institutes of the Christian Religion.* 2 vols. Edited by John T. MacNeill, translated by Ford Lewis Battles. Philadelphia: Westminster Press, 1960.

Carden, Allen D. *The Missouri Harmony.* Cincinnati: Morgan and Sanxay, 1833.

Chase, Gilbert. *America's Music: From the Pilgrims to the Present.* 3d ed. New York: McGraw-Hill, 1955; rev. 2d ed., 1966; rev. 3d ed., Urbana: University of Illinois Press, 1987.

Christmas in the New World. Musical Heritage Society recording, MHS 4077.

Claghorn, Charles Eugene. *Biographical Dictionary of American Music.* West Nyack, N.Y.: Parker Publishing, 1973.

Cobb, Buell E., Jr. *The Sacred Harp: A Tradition and Its Music.* Athens: University of Georgia, 1978.

Complete Works of William Billings. 4 vols. Edited by Karl Kroeger. Boston: American Musicological Society and Colonial Society of Massachusetts, 1981.

Cotton, John. *Singing of Psalmes a Gospel Ordinance. Or a Treatise wherein Are Handled These Foure Particulars. I. Touching the Duty Itselfe. II. Touching the Matter to Be Sung. III. Touching the Singers. IIII. Touching the Manner of Singing*. London: printed by M. S. for H. Allen and J. Rothwell, 1647. Extant copies may be found at both the New York and Boston Public Libraries.

Crouse, David L. "Allen D. Carden: Early Tennessee Musician." *Tennessee Historical Quarterly* 39, no. 1 (Spring 1980): 11-15.

Daniel, Ralph T. *The Anthem in New England before 1800.* Evanston, Ill.: Northwestern University Press, 1966; reprint, New York: Da Capo, 1979.

DeVenney, David P. *Nineteenth-Century American Choral Music: An Annotated Guide.* Berkeley, Calif.: Fallen Leaf Press, 1987.

Dox, Thurston J. *American Oratorios and Cantatas: A Catalog of Works Written in the United States from Colonial Times to 1985.* 2 vols. Metuchen, N.J.: Scarecrow Press, 1986.

Dunning, Albert. "Calvin [Cauvin], Jean." *The New Grove Dictionary of Music and Musicians*. Vol. 3. New York: Macmillan, 1980.

Elson, Louis D. *The History of American Music*. Rev. ed. New York: Macmillan, 1915.

Epstein, Dena J. "A White Origin for the Black Spiritual? An Invalid Theory and How It Grew." *American Music* 1 (Summer 1983):" 53-59.

Finck, Henry T. *Wagner and His Works*. Vol. 2. New York: Charles Scribner's Sons, 1904.

Hamm, Charles. *Music in the New World.* New York: Norton, 1983.

Haraszati, Zoltan. *The Enigma of the Bay Psalm Book.* University of Chicago, 1956.

Hastings, Thomas, and Solomon Warriner. *Musica Sacra.* Utica, N.Y.: William Williams, 1818.

Horn, David. *The Literature of American Music.* Metuchen, N.J.: Scarecrow Press, 1977.

Horn, Dorothy D. *Sing to Me of Heaven: A Study of Folk and Early American Materials in Three Old Harp Books.* Gainesville: University of Florida Press, 1970.

Jackson, G. P. *White Spirituals in the Southern Uplands.* Chapel Hill: University of North Carolina Press, 1933; reprint, New York: Dover, 1965.

Jubilee and Plantation Songs: Characteristic Favorites, as Sung by the Hampton Students, Jubilee Singers, Fisk University Students, and Other Concert Companies. Philadelphia: Oliver Ditson Company, 1915.

Krummel, D. W. *Bibliographical Handbook of American Music.* Urbana: University of Illinois Press, 1987.

Krummel, D. W., Jean Geil, Doris J. Dyen, and Deane L. Root. *Resources of American Music History.* Urbana: University of Illinois Press, 1981.

Law, Andrew. *The Art of Singing.* Cambridge, Mass.: W. Hilliard, 1803.

Little, William, and William Smith. *The Easy Instructor: Or, A New Method of Teaching.* Albany: Websters and Skinner and Daniel Steele [1811].

Lowens, Irving. *Music and Musicians in Early America.* New York: W.W. Norton & Company, 1964.

Lyon, James. *Urania.* Philadelphia: [printed by William Bradford], 1761.

Marsh, J. B. T. *The Story of the Jubilee Singers; With Their Songs.* New York: S. W. Green's Sons, 1883.

Mason, Lowell. *Carmina Sacra.* Boston: J. H. Wilkins & R. B. Carter, 1841.

_____. *The Choir.* Boston: Carter, Hendee and Co., 1833.

McKay, David P. "Cotton Mather's Unpublished Singing Sermon" *New England Quarterly* 48, no. 3 (September 1975): 410-22.

McKay, David P., and Richard Crawford. *William Billings of Boston: Eighteenth-Century Composer.* Princeton, N.J.: Princeton University Press, 1975.

Metcalf, Frank J. *American Writers and Compilers of Sacred Music.* New York: Abingdon Press, 1925.

Music in Colonial Massachusetts 1630-1820. II: Music in Homes and Churches. Boston: Colonial Society of Massachusetts, 1985.

The New Grove Dictionary of American Music [Amerigrove]. Edited by H. Wiley Hitchcock and Stanley Sadie. London: Macmillan, 1986.

Playford, John. *An Introduction to the Skill of Musick.* London: printed by W. Godbid for J. Playford, 1674. Reprint. Ridgewood, N.J.: Gregg Press, 1966.

Pratt, Waldo Seldon. *The Music of the Pilgrims.* Boston: Oliver Ditson, 1921.

Psalms of David. Translated from the Dutch by Francis Hopkinson. New York: James Parker, 1767.

Reese, Gustave. *Music in the Renaissance.* Rev. ed. New York: Norton, 1954, 1959.

Rivers of Delight. Nonesuch recording, H-71360.

Sacred Harp Singing. Library of Congress recording, AFS L11.

Sandburg, Carl. *The American Songbag.* New York: Harcourt, Brace and Co., 1927.

Sankey, Ira D., James McGranahan, and Geo. C. Stebbins. *Gospel Hymns: Nos. 1 to 6 Complete.* Cincinnati: John Church Co., 1894.

Schleifer, Martha Furman. "Centennial Exhibition." In *Amerigrove.*

_____. *William Wallace Gilchrist (1846-1916): A Moving Force in the Musical Life of Philadelphia.* Metuchen, N.J.: Scarecrow Press, 1985.

Schmidt, John C. *The Life and Works of John Knowles Paine.* Ann Arbor, Mich.: UMI Research Press, 1980.

Scholes, Percy. *The Puritans and Music in England and New England.* New York: Russell and Russell, 1962.

Seeger, Charles. "Contrapuntal Style in the Three-Voice Shape-Note Hymns of the United States." In *Studies in Musicology, 1935-1975.* Berkeley: University of California Press, 1977, 237-51.

Sewell, Samuel. *The Diary of Samuel Sewell, 1674-1729.* 2 vols. New York: Farrar, Straus and Giroux, 1973.

Shaped-Note Singing: A List of References. Library of Congress.

Sonneck, O. G. *Francis Hopkinson, the First American Poet-Composer (1737-1791), and James Lyon, Patriot, Preacher, Psalmodist (1735-1794); Two Studies in Early American Music.* Washington, D.C.: Printed for the author by H. L. McQueen, 1905.

Southern, Eileen. *Biographical Dictionary of Afro-American and African Musicians.* Westport, Conn.: Greenwood Press, 1982.

_____. *Music of Black Americans: A History*. 2d ed. New York: W. W. Norton & Company, 1983.

_____. "Musical Practices in Black Churches of Philadelphia and New York, ca. 1800-1844." *Journal of the American Musicological Society* 30, no. 2 (Summer 1977)): 296-312.

Stevens, John. *Music and Poetry in the Early Tudor Court.* New York: Cambridge University Press, 1961, 1979.

Stevenson, Robert. "America's First Black Music Historian." *Journal of the American Musicological Society* 26, no. 3 (Fall 1973): 383-404.

_____. "Gilchrist, William Wallace." In *Amerigrove.*

_____. *Protestant Church Music in America.* New York: Norton, 1966.

_____. "The Music that George Washington Knew: Neglected Phrases." *Inter-American Music Review* 5 (Fall 1982): 19-77.

Strunk, Oliver. "Zeuner, Charles." *Dictionary of American Biography.* New York: Scribners, 1936.

Sutton, Brett. "Shape-Note Tunebooks and Primitive Hymns." *Ethnomusicology* 26 (January 1982): 11-26.

Temperley, Nicholas. *The Music of the English Parish Church*. 2 vols. New York: Cambridge University Press, 1979.

Temperley, Nicholas, Howard Slenk, Margaret Munck, and John M. Barkley. "Psalmody (ii), *The New Grove Dictionary of Music and Musicians*. Vol. 15. New York: Macmillan, 1980.

Terry, Richard, ed. *Calvin's First Psalter* [1539]. London: Ernest Benn, 1932.

Tick, Judith. *American Women Composers before 1870.* Ann Arbor, Mich.: UMI Research Press, 1983.

Trotter, James M. *Music and Some Highly Musical People.* Boston: Lee and Shepard, Publishers, 1883. Reprint. New York: Johnson Reprint Co.,1968.

Wallaschek, Richard. *Primitive Music.* London: Longmans, Green and Co., 1893.